THE LOVE OF UNCERTAINTY

THE LOVE OF UNCERTAINTY

Steven Harrison

SENTIENT PUBLICATIONS

First Sentient Publications edition 2008

A paperback original

Cover design by Kim Johansen, Black Dog Design
Book design by Adam Schnitzmeier

Library of Congress Cataloging-in-Publication Data

Harrison, Steven, 1954-
   The love of uncertainty / Steven Harrison. -- 1st ed.
       p. cm.
   ISBN 978-1-59181-073-5
   1. Knowledge, Theory of. I. Title.
   BD161.H29 2008
   121'.6--dc22

                                        2008030856

Printed in the United States of America

10 9 8 7 6 5 4 3 2 1

SENTIENT PUBLICATIONS
A Limited Liability Company
1113 Spruce Street
Boulder, CO 80302
www.sentientpublications.com

CONTENTS

CONTENTS

FOREWORD

For the past ten years Steven Harrison has been holding dialogue groups around the world. They were an experiment, an exploration of the potential for accessing more than the limited point of view of the self. They had no set agenda—just the intention to express what was alive, vital, passionate, and true in the interactions of the participants. They took place in private homes, retreat centers, schools, bookstores, and auditoriums in the U.S, Europe, Africa, and India. At any one meeting, there could be only a handful, or hundreds of people in attendance.

What happens when a group comes together with no clearly defined purpose, no one shaping the experience, no shared belief system, and not even a yardstick for measuring success in the experiment? This may sound like chaos, and there were times when the dialogues were very lively and unformed. There were also times of boredom, argumentation, drama, laughter, and serene stillness. Just like life.

The dialogues were an attempt to do away with a prescribed form—or at least to make the form as transparent as possible—and let the movement of life create something new. And at times the individuals in the dialogue group stepped out of the way and allowed that to occur. In those moments the inquiry could move into extraordinarily thorny areas, including the nature of creativity, non-existence, exformation, group intelligence, positive confusion, the dynamic nature of not understanding, and the genesis of reality itself.

The intention behind this book was to give some of the flavor of that experiment, some of the liveliness of the interchange. But instead of a format with various people speaking, we decided to present the author's words, with the questions and comments of others occasionally folded into them for clarity's sake. The dialogues were group experiments and yet Steven Harrison was the one initiating, facilitating, and providing the strong impetus for those experiments. It is the wisdom of his words, eliciting and responding to the questions and comments of other participants, that you will find in these pages.

This is spoken language, albeit spoken by a very articulate person, so it carries a different character than written language. He often speaks in the first person to illustrate a point. In most cases, these illustrative first-person scenarios should not be taken to be autobiographical—they are simply a tool of expression.

A lot is packed into these short chapters, and they carry a perspective that our rational minds can find difficult to entertain. A slow reading is probably the best approach. It is my hope as editor that this book will convey something of the deep feeling underlying those meetings, and that readers will be moved by what they find here.

—*Connie Shaw*

PREFACE

When Connie Shaw brought up the notion of creating a book from talks and dialogs I have done over the past years, I found resistance to the idea. I felt that the words I had spoken in the discovery of what occurs at unformatted gatherings could not be taken out of the context of that meeting and those individuals. But much as I explore in this book, resistance is part and parcel of the creative movement, and I began to see that the transcripts were useful, not so much in their content, which is often imprecise and imperfect, but in the taste and feeling of inquiry. We stumble often as we look into the areas of life that are unfamiliar, and it is the willingness to continue on despite the impediments of unknowing that is portrayed here.

Do not look for a tight philosophical treatise in these pages, you will find only a partial record of the spontaneous exploration of the origins of our reality. Perhaps for you, this text will engender a deeper inspection of what you know about the world, and perhaps more interesting, what you can never know.

There are many co-creators of this book. My deep and heartfelt thanks to all those who have gathered over the years, taking the risk of creativity by stepping into an unknown space with me. Thanks, too, to those who organized the dialogs and brought me to all corners of the earth with no promise from me and no conditions placed on me. This book would not have occurred without the dogged insistence of Connie Shaw, along with her skilled editing, the relentless transcription of Adam Schnitzmeier, and Sentient Publications' dedication to publishing works of inquiry. And lastly, thanks to you the reader, for seeking this book and delving into this investigation of mind, consciousness, and reality.

—*Steven Harrison*

THE LOVE OF
UNCERTAINTY

WHAT IS CREATIVITY?

We seek creativity, the appearance of something that we haven't seen before. Yet what we see is described by what we have already seen. We encapsulate what we see into an experience based on what we already know, what we've already done. I wonder if we can have an experience that is not from the past, an experience that we have never had before.

If what you're experiencing now is known, then you know something about it—whether it's good or bad, agreeable or disagreeable. But if it's truly unknown, then what's also unknown is the knower: *who* you are, *where* you are, and *what* you are. You come into this moment presuming some things—that you're the body, you're the mind, you're the accumulation of experiences you've had, you're the future that you worry about. Or maybe you have the idea that you're none of those things, because you've read some books and had some experiences and you have the idea that you're consciousness, stillness, awareness or silence.

But in fact, if you have no idea *who* you are or *where* you are or *what* you are, then you can actually begin. That beginning is the point of creativity. It doesn't draw on what you know, it doesn't draw on what you are or your experience or skills. It's not located in you and it's not located in me. So *where* is it and *what* is it? Is creativity a feeling of flow, or a feeling of connection, a feeling of expression?

Let's look at how we *do* experience what's happening to us, and then let's see how we *don't* experience it. The way I experience a room I'm in is through information. I see the door, I see the windows. I see the look on the face of the other person in the room with me and I relate that look to other people who have looked like that in the past, and I bundle it all up into a "how's it going?" kind of feeling that tells me whether I should be more *this* or less *that*. That experience is happening both in a conceptual framework and in the body— the feeling of anticipation, the feeling of caution, tightness.

All very interesting, but I also notice that there's the rest of the universe. There's *my* experience, this little piece of it that is the *in*formation, but there's also the *ex*formation, *everything else*, which has been eliminated in that information. The exformation is much broader, bigger, more intense, and inclusive than my information. Once I see that, then I have a challenge, which is to look *around* the information to get at what's happening. The information just tells me a piece of what *did* happen, it doesn't tell me what *is* happening. I have to look at the exformation—the space around the information—to understand what's actually going on.

Is it possible to have an experience of what is around what we normally call experience, which is what we know?

Is some other kind of experience possible? Not in theory, but happening here and now.

I'm not interested in what *my* experience is. I'm really interested in what *our* experience, the *whole* experience is. I notice that I can't get to the whole experience through my experience. I'm intensely tired of my experience, as I hope you are. It's just been going around and around in circles. But how do I access *her* or *his* or *your* experience—the space around my particular historic, ideated experience?

All I know is the experience-gathering story, and that's repeating itself. Expectation is the prediction that experience gives us: "This is what happened *last* time, so this is what probably *will* happen." What stops the experiencer, ready or not, from encapsulating *everything* into more of the same? I prepare myself. I do my spiritual practices or my *post*-spiritual practices or my *non*-practice or my silence or whatever it is that I do—because I'm pretty good at doing *something*— and I'm prepared, and then something happens. That *something* automatically becomes experience.

But if we're not going for experience—whether we're ready or not—there's no way to even know what occurs. We know how to get ready for an experience, but if we're not interested in the realm of experience anymore, then how do we know anything about anything? How do we know what to *do* with that? This is the edge of what we know, and we sit on that edge, play on that edge. If everything on the edge is known, then I guess we have to unknow.

How do we recognize newness? How do we get from the repeating pattern that I call me and am so proud of, so defensive about, so aggressive with, and so in love with? This thing called me—wonderful, awful, whether with high self-esteem or low self-esteem—how do we get from that to *newness*?

3

Creativity comes out of the other side of destruction. Without destruction, nothing is created. There's just the past, repeating. We *apply* the past to the new, and cover it over. Our belief in the experientially referenced selves will be vaporized if we're actually *living* creatively, not just *talking* about living creatively.

What is creativity if I include the exformation? Here I am having my little subjective informational creativity when I notice that the whole experience is collapsing. Then a new experience emerges, and I think, "*That* is creativity." Now I have that little bubble of creativity that I've made, and there's the rest of the universe going on. Let's include information and exformation, and put it all together into something *total*. What's the creative movement then?

Perhaps we can be happy with a quasi-Buddhist description of thought arising and creating the universe, and that's it—we're pretty much done. We can just go practice watching or manifesting and that's it, because that's all there is. But if we're creating this little something out of nothing, then we're living in a subset of totality. Is that it? Is there any way to access a *total* quality *and* for that to be creative?

What human beings have recognized so far is that we cause experience out of totality, and that's all we can get to. Is there any other possibility? Can we function from something else besides that little experience machine, and even something other than the meta-level of the *recognition* of that experience machine? We not only have the experience, we also recognize that we're generating the experience, so we have our little awareness as the watcher of that experience.

The important question is *what* is creating wholeness and the expression of wholeness, and where do you sit in relation to that? Mostly where we sit is "I'm in a fragment having this experience of wholeness. And that's pretty darn good, because I *had* that experience, I *have* that experience, and I *will have* that experience, and that gives me something to hang my hat on—the experience of wholeness." But now we see that the experience is actually generated by the fragment arising and stripping out a piece of it, and the experience is just a little piece pretending to be the experience of the whole.

But is that true and is it creative and are we content to go about our apparently separate creative lives with this labyrinthine explanation?

It looks very much like we at least have the *idea* of separate doership. We certainly have a culture of separation; we express ourselves as separate beings. We all have our own driver's license or our bus pass, our personal possessions, our history, and all the rest of it. We seem to be expressing ourselves as if we're separate doers.

Then we have our spirituality, which is about generating an experience of the meta-level, a level of transcendence or God or connection. That meta-level is something we like to dabble in as an experience. We do our drug thing, our religious thing, or meditation thing or post-spirituality or *non*-spirituality, and we have that hit, our experience of the non-dual or the connected state. But it doesn't look like we want to *live* in that, to manifest from that, to express culture from that.

We're really good at manifesting something about *me* or *me and you*. We can get these small subsets going. I have the wife and the kid and the house and the job and that all works and I'm transcendent and hip. But it leaves out the other six and a half billion people, because I don't really care about them. They're not in my subset. What about the *whole?* What about manifesting something that is accessible, hip, interesting, transformative, and expressive of the *whole?*

PUSHING
THE RIVER

I don't mind pushing the river. I know that's not spiritually correct and I should be sitting and *watching* the river. Maybe I just need to revert to my former spiritual self who was able to just watch the river and think, "That's very cool." Sort of a Zen-like thing.

But what if I'm sitting by the river, appreciating the beauty of it, and in that Zen-like sensibility, I, the rock I'm sitting on, and the river all start to look like they're pretty much the same thing? Now does pushing the river take on a different characteristic than if I'm sitting *looking* at the object called *river*? If I *am* the river, don't I have the absolute universal right to push myself?

Shall we push the river? Why don't you and I, as parts of that river, *push* the damn thing? Why not? Is that a possible creative movement? Can life, the whole, the river, push itself?

Are we *interested* in pushing it? Otherwise we're just going to rationalize the life that we're already living. We go to Wal-Mart and we buy something and we feel good and substantial, our kid gets a report card, good and substantial, and we continue on in our life. But what if we think, "I am about to die" (which we could do literally or figuratively)? Now something completely new is about to emerge—molecular change—which *might* mean pushing whatever the river is.

Speaking as the river, and speaking as the one sitting and looking at the river—and anything else you want to name in that viewpoint—I feel like pushing the river.

Now what do I *do* with that? I could push those around me, which is my habit, my personality. But, I'm not really that interested in my habits anymore. I *am* interested in pushing the river.

Do you see the meta-level here? Do you absolutely think you are the location you've been assigned in this life that you're busy supporting? Are you really convinced that's true?

Can we just acknowledge we're the river, and then get on with what the river wants to create? That's a very interesting question, but we can't get there if we think we're sitting here watching the river.

I'm asking you to check in and see where you actually *are* located. If we think we're these locations, these subsets, then we'll be *that* I suppose. But we've been deconstructing the location thing for years now. At what point do we stop and say, "Okay, I'm not the location, I'm something unknown—the exformation and the information—so let's find out what the hell I'm going to *do* with *that*"?

Perhaps you feel that we're not pushing each other or

trying to push a metaphoric river, but we're just engaged in a process.

I am very suspicious of the word *process*.

Process implies time, which is a really interesting trap that we're constantly falling into. Time gives definition and location, and then we're in information. Time and information are the same thing. If we're in process, then we're in a location in the subset, and we can find out what that is. But if we're done with location and time, then all we really have to work with is manifestation—not then, and not before, but *currently*.

It's not going to be *me* pushing the river, it's *us*—the river—pushing, birthing, creating. I have no idea if this is the moment in which that occurs in some kind of spontaneous action, without any preconditions, including the idea that we must rid ourselves of our ideas.

The game of the ego is to have the idea of its own substance, and then it sets about destroying itself—analyzing itself, helping itself, rejecting itself. There's no ego to destroy. Sorry. If there's no ego to destroy, then the ego is the expression of the whole. Now you're the river—in your arrogance, in your stupidity, in your foolhardiness. That's the river.

We're not experiencing newness because we have the hazy illusion that we're individuals working on ourselves in time and process. But there is just manifestation. And you're it. And the you is not you, the you is we. That's all fine. Now I'm manifesting and you're manifesting, but is that *it?* The push is what I'm calling the creative expression. It's not pushing out of *you* though, it's pushing out of some broader base, because the push that is your habit doesn't have any energy anymore.

Perhaps you feel that your particular habits are safe, and

that an expression that is not habitual may involve doing things you don't want to do.

Creativity might mean doing *everything*, what you like and what you don't like.

Or maybe even worse, doing everything exactly the *same* as you now do it. There are no guarantees about the unknown.

If you look at the structures out of which we're functioning and habitually moving, as if there's just me and everything I collect around me for my particular enhancement, you see that, collectively and socially, the structures are tired out. They're not working. Look at the world and the way it's configuring itself. It's consuming itself in the individual search for security. That is expressing itself in the form of thought arising all the time, trying to collect security for each individual as if each individual can have security when the person next to them doesn't. On whatever level you want to view it, what's happening is the exhaustion of the manifest form that we've collectively and individually taken on.

If that's exhausting itself and fear arises—if *terror* arises—I say *that* energy *is* the creativity we're looking for. But what we call creativity is often a code word for feeling good—feeling the flow, or feeling like I'm doing something that's valued by myself or society. I'm saying creativity is *everything that expresses itself*, not just what feels good. When fear and terror starts coming up, that's it too. It means you're touching into the space that we're trying to explore and we can actually begin to explore it. We have all heard the advice on what to do with fear—breathe into it and so on. I have no *idea* what to do with it. I know what the habit is: pull back from fear and try to protect myself. But what I'm protecting myself from is energy, the creative force.

9

The exformation is *always* going to be overwhelming. It's always going to be experienced by this *in*formation as fear, because it's always going to be vastly greater than the information. We could say that fear is a portal to the exformation, the vastness, which is washing downriver and pushing. And what we tend to do, what the thought structure does, is try to cover our heads and hold back the flow.

We've all gotten quite enamored of energetically cool spaces. We've become very comfortable in awareness and silence. But they've become spaces; they've become experiences that we practice. The nature of life is that it breaks down all experience, because experience is always inaccurate. The crush of exformation is always pushing in against the information, and that's transformation. That's how change happens. Otherwise we would just have our information, it would repeat itself endlessly, and that would be that. It would be a static universe. But obviously it's a dynamic universe and change is occurring. How does change occur? Well originally we were in agitated states and we found peace. Okay, that's a change. Now that we've found peace and it's really nice, we can sit around and talk about it and know what we're talking about. We can create it, and special people have it—everything we call spirituality follows from that.

What we feel as a push is agitation, whether we call it an internal or external push, whether I'm manifesting that push and it's irritating *you* because you don't like to be pushed, or you are irritating *me* because I don't like someone telling me that I'm pushing them. It's all the agitation of change. It's destroying something and creating something. I have to make myself available to that even if it means that my persona—well-developed and well-positioned as it is—will be destroyed. Because the hunger is for the creative movement that comes through that destruction; and it's not two things, it's really one.

It's not that we need destructive energy or that we need fear or that we need anything in particular. But what *does* actually happen? When we come to the exposure of the exformation do we go with the moving energy or do we try to hold the river back? What happens? I find *that* fascinating—what actually happens.

Can we destroy ourselves and create ourselves? Are we here for that movement? And can we live like that? Maybe a better question is, *will* we live like that? Will we encounter each other like that? Or do we try to control the energy so that it has certain qualities, so that we have nice relationships, feel good, feel useful? Can we actually explore the full spectrum of the energy of life? Isn't that exploration creativity?

THE DINOSAUR AND THE COMET

As we attempt to communicate—which we usually think of as sending information back and forth between ourselves—it's interesting to look at the space around that information. What communicates is not information, it's exformation—the space around the information. What *doesn't* happen is the essential element of communication.

I don't know how we step into what we call creativity or whether creativity is just another idea, but the invitation is to step into that question. Do we mean by creativity something that *I* create and then transfer to *you*? Is it something like singing or dancing, or is it a whole thing, expressed in the whole space? Often the investigation of creativity gets translated into something like grabbing a guitar and singing a song, which is a kind of creativity, but one that we've already experienced.

Can we actualize from that large energetic space? I don't know what that means particularly, but I know it isn't going to come just from *me*. That would be like a personal creative edge—my limitation and expression—and I can try to enhance that particular expression. But when the comet hits earth and wipes out the dinosaurs, what is the value of being on the edge of dinosaur creativity? When the comet hits the earth, do you want to be understanding and actualizing on the dinosaur level or the universal level? As humans we have to ask, is it the human potential to step into the larger space, or are we already in it?

Let's go into the metaphor of the dinosaur and the cataclysmic comet. If the dinosaur is information and the cataclysm is exformation, does the dinosaur have the capacity to be greater than a dinosaur? Or is it only when it's stuck in information that it is limited by its structure? Are we stuck with the information called *me*, the separate self, because we believe in it? Is it because we have this stickiness to the information, rather than the recognition of the exformation, the whole, which is the exformation and the information together? The whole responds to the cataclysm by evolving life forms that can live in the new climate, but can the dinosaur change with such intelligence? Can we change with the intelligence of the whole?

It's not necessarily that I *can't* step into the whole, it's that I *don't* do it. This is what I notice. *I* don't do it, *you* don't do it, *we* don't do it. We all believe in the information that we have called *me* that I'm going to transfer to *you*, which you may or may not take into *your* information. And now we can say that we are in relationship and we can be creative together, play music together, we can talk—but it's still an informational relationship.

I'm suggesting that information is a byproduct of the whole. The information—I—poses myself as being essential and important. But in fact the information I know is so tiny and meaningless a fragment of the whole that it's a ridiculous assumption. I live in that assumption, and now I'm going to become creative in that assumption. This is where we all are—wondering how to become more creative as a meaningless fragment of a byproduct of the whole.

I don't really *know* anything, and if I don't know anything *in fact*, what happens? What's the exploration then? When the dinosaur looks up and sees the comet coming down, it doesn't help much to think, "I'm a dinosaur and I'm eating my leaves very creatively and that's a pretty bright thing up in the sky." Is there a space that includes *all* those things, and then how does the dinosaur live creatively in that space?

If we understand that it's not a *me and you* universe, if we discard that information, we then step into the exformation plus the information—the whole. Then what is created in that?

It's the exformation that is most interesting to me, the part that we'll never see and never know, that's not measurable. Do we have access to that *now* or are we the pieces, the dinosaurs saying, "That's a pretty interesting comet"? Does everybody have access to the cosmos, which includes the comet and the dinosaur—the space in which each of us sits? If so, then we can communicate it. Bring it forward. Energize it. Reveal it. *Do* something with it. Give some form to it.

The individual trying to understand or create is an individual neurosis. But I also suggest that something is happening in the space, in the silence itself, in the totality. And that *itself* is moving, it's dynamic. When I notice *that*, I see that this individual is a very incomplete and fragmentary reflection of that, which I know is not going to be more than a neurotic expression, however creative I can be. But the dynamic movement of the whole, that's really interesting. It is not just a frozen universe where we're all one. How do I explore the dynamic nature, how do I give expression to it? What are we going to *do* with it? What's the action?

You have to discard a lot of information to get to the exformation. The information, such as what my name is, suggests a huge amount of exformation, that is, all the names that I don't have. We use information to navigate, but we've discarded huge amounts of the universe to have the information that we use. We've built a whole society out of information.

Can we live and function and express using something that is more inclusive or greater than the information we currently function with? Do we live as the energy or do we live as the fragment, who recognizes the energy only because the energy blasts through us occasionally?

We may feel we have a choice about this, but the energy is making the choice and *we're* choiceless. The fragment is choiceless. The energy is what's choosing. This piece has the idea that it's making choices, but in fact it's a mechanical process. The choice is happening energetically, a quantum occurrence.

What shall we explore—how this mechanical thing has the illusion that it's making choices and maybe we could have a better mechanical thing going on? Or shall we explore the nature of the energy? We can't ask that question from the mechanical piece; we have to ask the question from the energy. We've spent far too many hours asking that question from the fragment, asking that question more or less intellectually or perceptually. Can we ask that question energetically? Can the energy ask that question? Or is it just "It's a manifest world, what manifests is what it is, energy does that, we're just the manifestation, and we can just relax and watch TV or whatever it is we like to do. People live and die, and I have nothing to do with any of that"?

Like you, I'm *always* trying to locate myself in time and space. Always. Absolutely. And my *failure* to do that successfully and consistently is my only blessing in life.

I'm aware and all that, *and* I notice that the universe doesn't give a damn about any of my experiences, because who cares about my silence and bliss but me? Only *I* care about that. Everyone else cares about *their* experience, their security, their family; and we can build some contracts with each other and say that we sort of care about each other unless you get in the way of what *I* care about, and then we break the contract.

People often tell me there's nothing to do, we shouldn't do anything, because we're choiceless and life is doing everything. I usually notice that we're doing something anyway. If life is in us then why can't I say *I'm* doing it? If I'm here then *I'm* doing it. We're playing this game that *it's* God and God's making me do it, and then I get to drop out of my own life.

Perhaps you're thinking you can't be operating from the Godhead because you've never had the experience of enlightenment. Nobody *does* have it, nobody *will* have it, and nobody *can* have it. All we can do is *talk* about enlightenment. We can conceptualize it based on our conditioning, which is sometimes beautiful conditioning, sometimes expansive conditioning, and so on. But there is no experience of enlightenment. When you stop qualifying what is happening—the energy that's occurring—as experience, then you just have energy. And you can't call that good, bad, or anything.

But are we there now? Otherwise we're talking hypothetically and it's just one more description, one more experience that we're filing in the conceptual file as the thing that I think about when I think about creativity. If we're truly going to explore what creativity is, then we have to *be* with that, to be in the energy without qualifications and see what happens.

But just as a warning, the Godhead may not be a beautiful place. It may not be the place that we imagined. If you're on that plane to the land of the virgins you may or may not get there. We'll find out the next second where you end up. We can't imagine the space that is acausal, amoral, without any consideration of qualities.

There's no *you* there in the place that you're defining as your collection of experiences, of your qualifications, of how you characterize the energy of life into something that is knowable, that you can recognize. If you don't qualify all that energy, then what's there?

There's no way to answer this question, because how would you *see* it, how would you *know* it? How would you know a quality that isn't characterized as good or bad? There's no way to know it.

The fact that qualities keep showing up is an expression of the dynamic nature of life—life isn't a static thing, it isn't "oneness." We don't get there. It isn't fixed. Stuff keeps spewing out of universal oneness.

We think information is important, but that's within a context of *another* idea. If we're talking about *my* building a business, *my* being an employee, *my* leaving my handprint on this side of the cave, then information is *very* useful. But if you break down that kind of thinking about information, unfortunately you will end up with information being meaningless, including the information that suggested information is useful. This is *all* within a context that is a belief system. This is hard for us to see because we're so information-bound, we're so enamored with our information—from our big information, "God is (fill in the blank)," to our little information, "I paid my utility bill the other day." Information is what we structure our whole reality around, and what we're talking about is not the possibility that information stops happening, because information and exformation *are* the totality, so it's going to keep going.

We're not trying to get rid of information, but we're looking at whether there's a different way to relate to the spewing of stuff by the universe. If you try to use information to access exformation, are you just converting that into *new* information? The question "Is that true?" simply converts the *old* information into *new* information, so that now I have a deeper understanding or a broader understanding. And now I've got the big understanding and you have the little understanding. Is that what we're doing with all this?

What if we just honestly recognize that this stuff *is* happening? That includes the big space and the little space—so-called meaning and our idea that it *is* meaning *and* our idea that it's *not* meaning. All this is just the stuff of the universe, it's happening as it happens. We don't have to organize it. Nobody has to be different. They don't have to be less neurotic or more enlightened; no deep understanding of an enlightenment experience is necessary, it's just what it is, *and* is there anything to do creatively in that space?

It's tempting to suggest that our biological machinery is set up to side-track ourselves into certain kinds of experiences. We can survive better feeling connected to each other; but that feeling of connection is actually just synaptic discharge, which we then take to be something special and grand because we build a conceptual framework around it.

For example, helping people makes you feel good, or sitting in meditation makes you feel oceanic. These are biological states—certain areas of the brain are lighting up. If you don't do anything at all you feel sad and disconnected, and that part of the brain lights up. Your impulse to do something comes out of the desire to have a better feeling, in the biological sense.

We're inside our synaptic system *imagining* that we're outside of it. This is why I'm deeply suspicious of experience, of *every* kind, because experience is what our brains are creating all the time.

I can convert whatever is taking place into an experiencer, in which case it's completely subjective. It's the bio-machinery, it's synaptic material. That's what I'm used to doing because it allows me to characterize what's out there and be able to manipulate it, to move through it, to survive in my life, which is presumably what the thought mechanism is about in our biological history.

The neurotic mind seems to just keep going, it keeps characterizing, keeps trying to understand. The height of the spiritual ideal is that I'm going to make some effort to stop the neurotic mind—stop, stop, stop, pound my head against the wall, sit on a cushion, and then finally… But that's also in a space—the space of *not* doing. I'm not going to do *anything* about the movement of mind. That spiritual non-doing is going on *and* the space of totality, which is outside of my doing or non-doing, is going on. There isn't any mechanism that makes an experience out of that whole. There's no language for it, no obvious way to utilize it.

Is that *it?* Are we just an experience machine encapsulated in protoplasm? Is there any quality of intelligence?

The individual human biology is generally not very interested in the energetic space. It's interested in *its* survival, *its* ideas. What is fascinating to me is that I've lost interest in that individual space and yet the individual space keeps churning away. It's not creative, and this engenders a different kind of consideration. There may be a few other people who have also lost interest in that individual conversion of everything into a fixed space, and perhaps we can explore something about the energetic space without creating a new cult, religion, or story.

To really explore means you have to *leave* the fixed space, which means stepping into a connected life, which is at best terrifying. It's something that we talk about but seldom actually *do*.

There never will be an explanation for that interconnected life. That's why it can never take the form of what we see in society, of a religion or a philosophy or a political movement or anything like that. It can never have that form. You can never hold on to it, you can only completely *live* it. It's paying attention to the space between the forms, the exformation as well as the information. It's the quality of total engagement.

THE MESSY WHOLE

To communicate with you I have to discard a great deal of exformation, resulting in the summary that is the words I'm using. You're going to take that into your system and summarize it into your own information, which is the result of the exformation that you've discarded to make meaning out of what I'm expressing.

Is it possible to communicate as human beings without speaking from the information, which is a piece that is left over when we discard everything else from the whole? We haven't developed the means to do that because the whole is messy. We don't know what to do with it, so we shrink it down to information, which gives us meaning—it gives *me* meaning, at least, and I don't care so much about whether it gives *you* meaning, but I'll try to convey my meaning to you. The messy whole has everything in it and I sort that out to decide that this piece of it is meaningful, and the rest of it I'm going to discard. That piece of information, "I'm a man, I'm a Christian, I'm an American," I then convey to you and then you convert it into something that has content for you. This is what we call communication.

Do we have any other capacity? Can we live in and speak from and receive in the *whole* or do we like the order that information gives us—the predictability, the known-ness of it? There's actually *more* information in the mess than there is in the order. But we tend to go toward the order because it's a knowable quality, it's predictable, it's safe.

A messy kitchen has more information than the kitchen that has been all cleaned up and is all in order, but we don't like the mess. The information in the order—the toaster goes *there*—is the result of discarding a lot of other information: all the places the toaster *doesn't* go. That has meaning to us because it tells us where the toaster *should* be, but it doesn't necessarily have creativity, because we'll never know what happens if the toaster is in the other fifty thousand possible positions in the kitchen.

Time is also a kind of information—sequenced information. At this moment we're disregarding all other moments.

When we communicate with each other, what's actually happening? I bring a perception that I'm having into a series of words, hoping to insert it into your brain where it's going to become the experience that I'm having, but in your brain. I may think I'm going to make something clear to you, but what does it mean to gain clarity? How would you know if you gained clarity by something that I say to you?

What are we trying to produce as we communicate with each other? Is it a feeling-state? The feeling of flow, the feeling of completeness, the feeling of connection, the feeling of wholeness? Is it a meaningful state in which I think, "Ah, what *you* say fits into what *I meant?*" and therefore I have constructed greater meaning because now we share that meaning.

For example, we could all declare ourselves inquirers, and create the new Church of Inquiry. We sit in a circle, we ask the ten questions, we respond to them in a deep way, and that is the Church of Inquiry. We've established meaning; we've *expanded* the sense of meaning.

Are we constantly trying to reduce the whole to an experience that fits into the world view that we hold? We establish that over and over and over again. Or is it possible to not *have* a world view, to not have a construction, to not make meaning out of this, and still communicate and still discover? What is that quality? What comes of that?

In a sense, we have to discard whatever information we build out of our interactions. That could suggest to some of us that what is left when we discard the information, and the response to it, is just silence. We like silence, and so we think, "*That's* the result." We like that formulation and we like the silence experience where we subtract the information that comes in, we subtract our response, and we go into a silent space. But let's be very precise—silence is *also* a form of information. It's also something that we build meaning around, so now we can say we're the Church of Silence. We practice this just like Catholics practice their particular rituals or Buddhists practice *their* particular rituals. We're ritualizing silence. Can we discard silence and whatever meaning we give to it? Why do we concern ourselves with silence anyway? Why do we find that interesting or worthy of focus?

The importance of silence is a trick someone's played on us. I don't know about the silence. Go into the feeling, give expression to the feeling. We don't have to go into the silence, the silence is a lie. This is a state of mind being practiced by spiritual people and it's just something we measure ourselves by—because if we're not silent we must *really* be terrible people.

Can you stay with your feeling and not describe it? Not call it pain or fear? Not call it anything in particular? Just feel it and give expression to the feeling continuously. Then you can report back your findings to people with whom you are in relationship. Can you simply feel and give expression to feeling without description?

The qualities that we're calling pain, life, and energy are all the same. Can this quality of feeling and the expression of it without the description be continuous?

A World of Summaries

Information is the summary of all possible manifestation. If you take your entire life experience up to this point and discard that to ask the question "What is information?"—that's a piece of information. That tells me something about *you*—you're not asking about your childhood, when you were seven and something happened; you're not asking about what happened this morning. You're not referring to anything but this one question. That requires discarding all your information, which is exformation once you discard it, to have a piece of information. It's a summary. We're all summarizing, because if we try to express totality at all times, well, we wouldn't know what that would be like. We have used the term *silence* to approximate totality. "The expression of everything is nothing" is the spiritual shorthand for that. But when we actually try to live in a life, then we end up summarizing to function. That summary is information, and that becomes identity—me and you, who I am and who you are, our history and where we're going in the future. This whole construction out of information has become a burden.

Information plus exformation is the whole. If you summarize whatever totality is, that's information, and that information is not the whole. It is an approximation and a poor one at that. To summarize you have to take something very large and expansive and bring it into something very small. In our developed world we think that information is an accurate representation of the universe. We use information as a technology, a way of functioning, building, and creating culture and communication and relationship. The question occurring now—perhaps in the culture as a whole—is "Is that *all?*" Is that the total capacity of the human being, to summarize everything and center oneself in that summary, and then relate to each other as if that summary is accurate?

We seem to somehow know that the summary isn't accurate—it's just a tool we use to function. The tool, though, becomes so real that it gets in the way, because now we *do* believe that "I'm a man, an American," and that "you're a woman and a Canadian." There's a whole world out there having wars and disputes over these *ideas*—"He's a Muslim, he's a Christian, he's an American, he's an Iraqi."

We can see that we live in something like virtual reality, and we can see that simultaneously there is something we call awareness. This was a breakthrough at some point. But now awareness has become something else, a "thing." That thing has all kinds of attributes we talk about as if it's the same thing for all of us. Now we've got a new level of the virtual reality world. I'm suspicious of the idea of awareness, silence, or wholeness, because now people are having that experience and practicing that experience with each other. Now we can refer to that experience together, just like someone who believes in Jesus will refer to their personal relationship to Jesus, or a Buddhist refers to Buddha or the Buddha-mind. These are things that are meaningful within that virtual reality. Maybe silence or consciousness is meaningful to some people, but this seems to me to be just one more thought form, one more piece of information.

We can see that all these pieces of information are fixed; these summaries are fixed. They don't have creativity in them. If we build a world from summaries, from information, *that* world doesn't have creativity in it either. We can move those pieces around a lot, but they're the same pieces. If we add silence or consciousness to that, we have another piece, but it's still not creative.

If we're ornithologists we might study sparrows and come to believe that we can interpret their cheeping. We begin to transcribe their cheeping and of course learn how to cheep so they'll cheep back—then we have entire relationships with the sparrows. "Hello, welcome back, how's the house? That's very nice. How are the kids? That's great." This world really starts to develop because we believe that this cheeping has meaning. If we step back from that we can see that the sparrows *do* make noise and it may have some relationship to their biology, it may even express some communication, even if it doesn't have any intrinsic content. So when we think that the expression of totality can't happen with words, I'm going to ask why not? Why can't the words be a by-product of something happening? We are missing the point if we think that the significance is *inside* the words.

Usually at this point we all decide that it's not in the

words and we go into the silence and we have an experience of non-verbal oceanic feeling, and we think, *"That's it."* Then we go back out into our lives and we start talking about it. Or if we can be really quiet then maybe people come, project their spiritual fantasies on us, and pay us for our quiet.

But functionally we *do* talk.

Can we see if there is something else going on that is not what we would normally assign meaning to? I don't know if that means we have to not assign meaning to the words we use or that we have to *enhance* the meaning, we have to expand how that meaning is understood. This is the experiment. What we're really exploring is the potential. What does happen if we *don't* push it all into the information level and at the same time we don't become abnormal, we don't take on special qualities, we're not spiritual or expanded or enlightened? We're just *here* and still communicating. What actually takes place?

THE END OF IDEALISM

Awareness is actually a thought form. Maybe it's a higher order of thought form, maybe it's a more inclusive thought just like the thought of a group is a more inclusive thought than the thought of "me." But it's still a descriptive thought.

We have a subtle formulation going on in our spirituality, which is that you're supposed to get to a place where mind is inactive. If we get there, that's significant. And here we are *now*, in fragmentation, which we don't consider a great place, hoping for the totality, which we have heard is a great space. But when we touch the totality we try to find *my* experience, and to see if *I* individually feel okay, "*I'm* okay, therefore *it's* okay."

We give up trying and just pay attention. We reside in our awareness. It is very relaxing to just sit here and watch the display of thought and feeling, without the brain having to do anything in particular. It's relaxing *and* it's also a thought form. Clear seeing, awareness of the phenomena, is just another form of thought.

There is the information in the words you speak and there is also an energetic component. If as you speak, the quality actually *occurs*, then there is a total meaning in the communication. If it's just packaged into the word and goes into my brain, then it's limited to information. Communication requires a component that we're not used to functioning with in our world—our speaking, our living, our expression can have an energetic component that is lined up with the words. Otherwise it becomes the *idea* of clear seeing or awareness. If clear seeing is a fact in your expression, then clear seeing is automatically conveyed to those with whom you're communicating. Or I would have to say it's *not* a fact, and the information is disconnected from the whole.

Can the words, the information, be totally lined up with the energetic reality? That *does* require the end of idealism. Clear seeing isn't the ideal that we are trying to achieve. We're going to constantly convince ourselves that we're in a state of clear seeing when actually we're in the *thought* or the *idea* of awareness, disconnected from the life in front of us. If there's no idealism about what we're doing then the expression is automatically the expression of the totality. But that doesn't have a particular form. We're all trying to place a form on the circumstance, on the energy.

That expression is always happening anyway—we represent that expression to ourselves in very disconnected ways, which is also an expression. You could say that the energetic expression then is disconnection.

Can the words we use (and for that matter any other

expression—our body language, movement, anything else) actually be an expression of the energetic movement? We can see this in very primitive forms in children. When a group with children in it becomes fragmented, they aren't able to sit still. They start to move in the chaos of the energy of the disconnection. On the other hand, in a very still space they tend to fold into that stillness and will probably fall asleep. They're not able to go out and build companies and so on because they don't have the intellectual development, but they seem to be flowing with the energetic reality. As adults, we have lost the energetic reality and have a hyper-intellectual movement going on.

The invitation is to line up the energetic flow—the movement of the space that you experience—with your expression, so that they're the same thing. Then we're not constantly disconnecting from the totality, the energy, using *my* virtual reality and then trying to connect to *your* virtual reality so that we've got a *new* virtual reality called our culture of this morning, or extended into time as our culture of next week and last week. Is it possible to have an energetic culture that is constantly reinventing itself? What would that be like? Is that a form of insanity? Is that a form of creativity? Or both?

Description requires us to discard almost *all* of the actual. The words don't really capture what we're trying to describe. We cannot convey whatever is occurring; we can only convey some pieces of it that we think are essential. We have to throw away all the non-essential to describe anything at all. That process, which is bound up in language, thinking, conceptualization, is what I'm calling information. You reduce the actuality to information within yourself and then you think, "That's my experience." But you've discarded most of it. What if you *don't* discard most of it? Is it possible for you to use words as a byproduct of conveying the whole? Then we're in the same energetic movement.

Words are a summary, but if they're a side effect of an energetic flow then they're not in the way. Words are not a problem, but they're also not the essential part. When words don't carry energy—the fullness of the quality that is attempting to move—then we become disassociated. That disassociation is also energy—it's what we call fragmentation. When we have the quality of disconnection or fragmentation and we use words to try to put it back together and it's just not going anywhere, we could call that an argument or a conflict.

The fundamental flaw with the idea that information is functional, that I might incorporate information that you're expressing into my world, is that it suggests two worlds—the world that you're occupying and the world that I'm occupying. Neither of those worlds exists. Those are summaries that we're throwing at each other. The world that *actually* exists is a synthesis of everything.

THE PLAY IS OVER

I'm interested in the whole illusion of "getting it." If I get it and I *have* it, then I'll have to convey it to the person who *doesn't* have it, and this is the beginning of a religious movement. The illusion is that my experience, which I bundle up and think is "it" (whatever it is, as beautiful as it is), becomes something that you *don't* have. I'm suggesting that we all have "it," whatever it is, because the "it" is the energetic movement, not some understanding, experience or realization that stands outside of that energy.

We search in the language database for the summary that has meaning, and we don't need to do that because that is the completely wrong direction. Go *into* the energetic field and let *it* express whatever *it* wants to express—words or no words, movement or no movement, walking out, standing still, whatever it is. The energy of the space, of the *world*, is expressing *itself* through these words now. But we have an imaginary world in which we search around for the word and that world is always going to be a particular reality, which you may or may not share. We have either agreement or disagreement in that world, so I'm always looking for the word that will convey to you something that would make you agree with *my* world. That's the whole point.

It's like saying "I wouldn't be like a conservative because I'm a liberal." Well that's great if you're a liberal. If I'm a Unitarian then everybody can be enfolded into *that*, and I am satisfied that's better than being a Catholic where you have to be a particular way. But those are both "ways." Everybody thinks *their* way is "the way" but it's not a way, it's just something else, some other reality—that's the nature of our construction.

Now we think, "Don't try to understand, let it be." It's a form of idealism to think that we should just let it be, that we shouldn't try to understand it—because some of us *are* trying to understand it, and some of us are trying to let it be. The energy is both of those things. Maybe it's the tension between those things or the energy created by those things.

What would our world be like if we spent less effort making agreements about what we see and touch and say, if we allowed the energy to be creative? I'm not just challenging us to ponder that, I'm challenging us to *be* it. *To be it here, now.* Another trap is the pondering and challenging of "What if? What would this be?" There's lots of places to go and talk about "it" and ponder "it" and express "it," but I'm interested in the *manifestation* of that quality. I'm interested in what happens when people come together and begin to deconstruct the way they hold reality.

What appears to happen so far is people deconstruct and

then they reconstruct again and then they come back to another retreat or another dialogue and deconstruct, and then start all over. I don't know if there is in fact a deep desire, a need, or expression of the deconstructed reality that we're all very interested in, and we want to explore that. We can ponder it, but ultimately we are what we actually manifest—and not as just the collection of individual pieces expressing the energy, but *as* the energy.

You enter a world in which you lose the capacity to assign meaning. You *can* attempt to assign meaning but it becomes a burden of constantly having to figure out meaning and understanding what that meaning is. But if you don't assign meaning to the flow of thoughts or feelings or energies going on then where *do* you stand and how *do* you function? This is a very radical relationship to the energy of life, and we'd like to have that containerized into "silence" or "awareness" because these are pretty safe areas. We go do a Vipassana retreat and we become aware and we watch our mind, and we can relax and be more effective at our job.

But I would suggest that an energetic life may be the *end* of your job or your marriage or your home and all the things that you think of as safe and secure. And it may *not*—it may mean you have to stay with your wife and your house and your job *forever*. We don't know. When we ask that question, are we really interested in that expression—are we moving as the energy moves in all ways? I find it to be a radical question in my own existence and I find tremendous resistances to that energetic movement.

We've modeled that if we can just hold our reality together and forget what's next so we can survive it, then that will bring us to safety. Like the man who went to the psychiatrist and said, "I'm afraid I'm going to die." And the psychiatrist reassured him, "That's the last thing you're going to do."

Letting go of our narrative is the *last* thing we are going to do. What we're constantly telling ourselves is, "It's the *last* thing—until then I'm going to go to the job and get the money and pay the mortgage and keep the marriage together and raise the kids. Because the *last* thing I'm going to do is die."

Not having a narrative holding our reality together destroys the notion of the movement of time, and then there's no predictability, there's no good and bad. From the perspective of the thought construction, that's terrifying. If I look at that energy from the "me" and everything that I've built up around that, then that excitement or energy is terror, because it's unpredictable. The totality is not in the present moment that I can get to, because *that* present, the invented present of the spiritual world where we're "in the moment," that's the past, it's already happened, I've already constructed around that experience. The present I'm talking about is the present I *can't* get to. That means there's *no way of knowing anything.* For the knower who wants to know everything and wants to have that knowledge protect itself—that "not knowing anything" is synthesized into fear.

The knower is the experiencer who wants to capture the moving energy into something fixed. I will attempt to control by storytelling, expressing meaning, convincing, excluding, overpowering—there's a long list there—all of which gives me the sense that I'm in control of *something*. That sense of being in control, imaginary as it is, is soothing. It's like I don't have a girlfriend but I go to a movie about a romance, and for a couple of hours I have a girlfriend. Then that's a good enough reason not to have a real girlfriend, even though I'm lonely. A movie is close enough to a life.

Dying is the *last* thing I do. This is how we get through it all.

We think we need to pay attention to thought, to see that thoughts occur in us and that we identify with them, and to see that we're conditioned to think that we're doing the thinking. We imagine that we need to watch carefully, and then awareness follows that, and then we can realize that it's nonpersonal.

But when you see that you're not "you," then what's left is that you're the universe. It doesn't change the question of manifestation. You can't just duck out and say, "Well it's the *universe* doing it so there's no responsibility; I'm just an empty shell." Because what's left is the whole and you're it.

What are you going to create next? The answer to that is what you *do* create next, what *we* create next, what is manifesting. We think that we need to be careful not to grab on to the mind, and I'm saying as *the Godhead,* you *can* grab on if you want. So go ahead and grab on.

We think there's a subtle difference between identifying with the thinking and saying "I" think, as opposed to being aware that it is thinking that's happening. That insight was then, and it was an insight when it was an insight, but once you *have* that insight it's no longer an insight—now it's a thought-form that's practicing itself. Once you've had that insight, you're the flow of whatever that is, and if you grab on to a thought, then you do.

Before you knew the difference between identifying with thought and identifying with the awareness of thought, maybe it was important to stay awake and aware of the difference. But now that you know, why is it important to stay awake and aware? I don't make *any* attempt to be awake or aware *at all* in my life.

I do remember having the idea at one point in my life that I should be awake and aware—it's a tremendous pressure—

and I did find myself being quite awake and aware and I was pretty impressed with that and so were the people around me. But at a certain point that became an idea or a practice that was its own story, it was like a thought bubble. Then I asked the question, "What would it mean to be *un*aware?" I tried really hard to *not* be aware and I came to find out that I couldn't force myself to *not* be aware. Then you have to think, "Well, something else is happening. Okay, I *am* awareness or whatever the hell it is."

You're expending all this energy in being aware, but what's the fear? If you're *not* aware, if you're caught up in thought, what happens? It's like Shakespeare said—all the world's a stage and we are just players on it. When you're caught up in thought, you're caught up in the play. You think there's some value to being aware that it's a play.

Try to give up awareness and get back into the play. Good luck. The only echo of that whole thing in your mind is the idea that you have to *do* something to not be in the play— and I'm telling you *the play is over,* you can't get back into it. When you're in the play and then pop out of it, for the first moment you go, "Oh that's awareness, and now I'm aware that I'm in the play." But that was then and this is now.

I don't feel like I have to be careful and here's why: If I were just me living in my world, I would have to be really careful, but I'm living with *you.* And I know that if *I* go down the wrong path, *you're* going to say, "Hey, that's the wrong path." I'm in relationship to so many hyper-vigilant, intelligent, and insightful human beings that *I don't have to be careful.* It's beautiful.

At one point I constructed myself *as* the play, and then I learned meditation and philosophy and something called "awareness" where I *watched* the play. *Both* of those are stories. Wherever you are in the story it's the same question, which is can you drop the story and live? Can you line up the energetic field—which is not a personal experience and not about *me*—with the personal, which is my expression? I own my expression personally as the field, not me trying to *get* to the field. The story is how I got the field, the wholeness, and then I dropped back in experience, which made me better, and I'll tell you about it, and we tell each other about our experience of the whole. But the whole doesn't *have* an experience—it *is* the experience.

We're the manifestation of the whole and we can't get to the whole through the perspective of the part. We *are* there.

Where we are is usually a description of where we *should* be or an idealization of where we are, like "this is the silence and that's wonderful" or "we should be in less conflict." But *where we are* is already *happening*. What if we start to build our relationship, our language, our culture around the energetic reality rather than the disconnected intellectual conception? I'm not discarding the conceptual framework at all; it's still a useful tool. It's a piece of information alongside the exformation.

I'm posing the question of whether the human being at this point is interested in exploring creativity rather than rehashing the past—and that means *manifesting* creativity, not talking about it or pondering it but actually *doing* it. That means how we live, how we relate to each other, how we form our marriages, how we raise our children, how we deal with businesses—what we're doing with the world *as it is*, whatever that is. We have not gotten to the world as it is, only our imaginings.

FREEFALLING

When scientists study how much sensory information we're taking in they count it in millions of bits of information, but we may be aware of only ten to forty bits of that information.

We thought awareness was going to do it for us, but the most we seem to be able to be aware of is a tiny *fraction* of what's actually happening. Just pay attention to the bottom of your feet now and feel the pressure. That pulse and sensation probably wasn't part of your awareness until I directed it there. So the question of happiness is an interesting one, because maybe we already *are* happy and we just don't know it because we're paying attention to something else—like the bills that aren't paid or the argument we just had.

Metaphorically, the question of where our attention or our awareness is, is really the same as asking how we construct our reality. We talk about awareness as if it's of a different order than the ideas we have—but awareness *itself* is an idea. What to do with sorrow and what to do with happiness is really the same question.

We can construct happiness all the time—the price is dullness. We can do that through spirituality, by living in the "now." But *now* is surrounded by millions of other bits of information that we're *not* taking in—to have the so-called now that we feel is better to have than not to have.

The total now is so far beyond "better" and "worse" because it's beyond our actual capacity. Our human capacity to take it in is limited to this very small piece of it, so when we construct the feeling of now-ness we are also constructing an illusion.

We have to construct qualities such as happiness and sorrow out of our forty bits of information that we get to scoop out of the millions of bits that we can take in with our body senses, which are only part of the unknown, uncountable bits of information floating around. If we don't create these qualities, then *now* doesn't contain them. We do that because we'd rather have happiness and sorrow than the unknown, the unattainable, the untouchable, the ineffable.

Do we *have* to construct meaning—our forty bits of information, our little drop of reality—out of totality? Do we have to do that to function, to have meaning, to have a sense of identity—or is there the potential in the human being to live *fully* in the totality, without needing to construct the good and the bad, the happy and the unhappy? So far in history we've had to construct the social and political contracts and all the other structures to give ourselves identity, but those too seem to be breaking down.

We're all freefalling. We can construct anything we'd like in the midst of that freefall—our own imaginary world with our experience of happiness or unhappiness. Whether we do that or not doesn't change the fact of the immense energetic flow of the universe that's beyond our ability to capture by means of the faculties that we're used to employing.

And yet we don't have the capacity to actually live the freefall. Whether we say yes or no to it is irrelevant. If there's a wake up, it's really to the total irrelevance of anything we could possibly say or do in the face of the overwhelming on-slaught of bits.

We continue to weave story within story, like nested Russian dolls. We have a breakthrough and we create a new story about that, then if that breaks down we create a new story about *that*. But it's not easy to construct a story around the irrelevance of our story.

Not that it's depressing or self-destructive or bad or any of those negative connotations either. Irrelevance simply means that all the *stuff* that we're churning around with this forty-bit machine of ours is like an ant walking across a road. The ant is not particularly relevant to the traffic going down the street, although the ant may think it is and *you* may think you are relevant in your life.

In the face of totality we want to do something with the little piece we get each moment, so we string those pieces together into a coherent story. I can understand why we do that because otherwise we'd probably just be sitting around in awe, just complete awe. But then we're in the good and the bad and the ups and downs and all the story and drama, and we work our way through it, and we have the "aha" moments where we feel good about the story that we've woven. *That* story—the ups and downs and breakthroughs, the enlighten-ments—is *all irrelevant*.

That is the beginning point of something else. Our irrel-evance is an introduction to the immensity. The immensity is beyond the word "immensity" and beyond our capacity. I have no idea what that something else is because that would just be a story about beginning, but it doesn't have to do with my description or the narrative or the meaning of where I locate that something else. It's not that *you're* the enlightened one, *I'm* the enlightened one, *we're* the enlightened ones, or wherever we try to locate it. It doesn't have anything to do with *any* of that. It has something to do with what manifests, what *actually occurs*.

But we don't have access to what occurs. We don't have the ability to measure the energetic manifestation. It would be like going to the Empire State Building with a ruler and measuring a foot because that's as far as our ruler goes. Our toolbox is pretty limited, and what we're using just doesn't have that capacity. Now we might say to ourselves that we *collectively* have more capacity, so if we take all of us, and that's maybe forty bits times fifteen, or fifty, or five hundred, or five million, then wow, the capacity's really going to be there. But it still doesn't quite do it.

Perhaps we have the capacity to see those forty bits more clearly as a group of people, but "more clearly" often just shows that it's limited. That's the basic *unclarity*—that I think my forty bits is actuality, you think yours is, and together we can see that *neither* is. This is where we get into the area of exformation, the space around the information. We have capacity for only forty bits, but that is a representation of everything we've discarded, which is everything else. The actual is in that meta-space, the space *around* and *including* the forty bits. It's not just in what I *think* about it but in everything else, too. It's like stepping into the space around the reality we're creating all the time.

We try to make this into meaningful information that passes between us. But I don't know that what I have to say is actually meaningful. Here *nothing* has meaning. If we're not looking for meaning, what will we find? If we don't try to construct meaning out of what I'm saying or what you're saying, then what is actually occurring?

Focused on the Forty Bits

When something difficult happens, we think we need to accept what is and move on. This "accepting what is" business translates into *constructing* what is. We have learned to neutralize what the energetic movement is in our world with the idea of accepting what is. Accepting what is means constructing something that doesn't tear my life apart.

What do I do when *my* "what is" is irritation with *you?* Do I accept it or do I express irritation? Should I accept it, whatever it is? When we accept what is, are we giving up the scooping out of the little clusters of bits of information, or do we continue to do that but we just have a cleverer name for it?

What do we *do* with all the acceptance? Are we actually doing nothing? Are we *living* like that? Is everyone just sitting around not acting? No, we're all acting, there's movement taking place. Some of that movement is reactive, some of it is passive—there are all kinds of different qualities.

How many bits of information are there in the universe? Whatever the brain is picking up—left brain, right brain, all brain, all of us holding hands saying Om—it's going to be an insignificant piece of totality, no matter how we cut it. A bit of information is a distinction, it's a separation of the universe into two things, like "male" or "female." It's a separation. No matter *what* our capacity is, we're always going to be facing our lack relative to the universe.

We have what arises in awareness and we have awareness, which we posit as something which is "outside of." But awareness itself is actually a limited, and limiting, factor. This is where the question of how many bits we can be aware of is significant, because we can be aware of only, let's say, a million and forty bits, if we use both sides of our brain *and* we hold hands with a whole lot of people. Our awareness is limited; it has capacity for only so much information. We've learned that awareness is a special thing that's unlimited and oceanic and cool, and we work with what arises, and *that's* the universe.

Here's what we do with awareness—the element of *thinking about our thinking* has become the entity called "me." That's who I am. I'm thinking about my thinking. My awareness, my specialness about this thought arising, is the entity called "me." Now I talk about me and everything I'm aware of as if that's important, as if it's accurate, as if it has some significance.

Let's just step theoretically and momentarily into the universal viewpoint, in which the thought of the thought is a bit of information, just like the *thought* is a bit of information, in a flow of untold, unlimited bits of information. The idea of "me" is also a bit of information. We're functioning from these bits as if that's the world. If one of those forty bits is the idea of a thinker, of a "me" who's aware of the other thirty-nine bits, then we have a *macro-bit* that is significant to me, but not to anybody else.

Now we've gone one step beyond that—now we've created bits of information that say we're *not* separate. So it's a unified universe and now you and I share *that* bit, and we have the idea of non-separation, which is of a larger order than the awareness of the thought process.

How many layers are we going to have before we just stop layering and look at some other way of functioning, experiencing, and expressing? We're just playing with these bits. I don't see a difference between the idea "I'm a thief," the idea "I'm *aware* that I'm a thief," and the idea "You and I are one (and I'm a thief, and your wallet is gone)." All thought-forms are floating around, and some of them are more acceptable. We create cultures of acceptability. In some cultures what we're talking about would be blasphemy and would be an unacceptable way of interacting, and we'd be *dead*. In other places this is very refined and very sophisticated material. We can meet and construct experiences—silence, peacefulness, oceanic, now. We can gaze into each other's eyes and feel love. We could do that and be silent for two hours, then go back to our slash-and-burn existence, and then come back next week and recreate love and silence again. We could even try to create a culture of love, in which we stare constantly at each other, and create some kind of holistic business of love—natural soaps or something like that. (That would be a good idea; maybe we should call a meeting.) And there's nothing particularly better or worse than those things. It's all of the same quality.

Have we seen that we don't have the capacity to access the whole thing? It's not that we're not willing or wanting to, or that we don't have all kinds of reasons to, but we don't actually have the *capacity* to. Yet we still have the idea that we *are* this forty-bit capacity. We struggle with this forty-bit capacity, trying to have some relationship to the whole show. Why do we still believe that we are the forty bits? Why is the question still held within that particular container?

Let's not go back to it. We know the whole is not there. Whatever that little bit of information is that I have, I know it is not going to tell me a damn thing about anything, other than my forty bits—a very, very small world, pretty irrelevant, pretty tired, pretty bored. Why would I reference that? I'm not saying it should go away, because it's *not* going to go away; it's part of the immense stream of information and exformation. But at what point do I stand in the universal and ask that question?

Without those forty bits there *is* no experience. Each time we refer to "experience" we're talking about time, meaning and location. If we don't take the forty bits out of the stream, we don't have an experience. If we don't have an experience, we don't have an *experiencer*. We can name that stream—we can call it "energy"—but it's not knowable, it's not doable, it's not me, it's not you, and it's not even "what is." It's just not even on the radar screen of what we can do with forty bits. If *that's what's actually happening*, why isn't that our reference point?

Doesn't that change the discussion we're having? The discussion we're having as a culture has no end to it. It's just going to go back into the forty bits over and over and over again, and we're going to constantly come to this question: How does the forty bits experience trillions of quadrillions of bits?

It doesn't have the capacity, won't *ever* have the capacity, and at the same time it creates the sense of self, which is simply another bit of information. We created this endless loop of referencing that has no end, but it's also a very, very *tiny* world that is not true.

Why are we functioning in the forty bits if we have everything else? I'm not particularly obsessed with the limitation of the forty bits, but perhaps I *am* obsessed with the question of whether that's a *true* limitation. Have we just gotten used to it, talked ourselves into it, trained ourselves, educated ourselves about it? We talk to each other as if it's true, and we've rewarded ourselves for that forty bits. If I can be very focused on *my* information and drive it through the culture—which is another piece of information—then I'm rewarded for that. We've created a whole world based on that dynamic, yet there's a vastness that we *don't* explore, we *don't* live in, we *don't* express culturally or interpersonally. What about that?

Isn't there something else to *do?* The action is where the action *is.* At the same time, I recognize that the way I describe that action brings it back inside the forty bits. My description of it is not going to be "it." The action, the doing, the energetic movement, is not going to be in the information. It's going to be in the totality.

Maybe it's a new level of information that we don't know about, and that is functional. For example, a group dynamic is a level of information that might be more functional than the individual level. Mostly groups are taken over by individuals—an individual who collects the group energy. Historically this is what has happened. We've never seen any evidence of group intelligence *functioning* as group intelligence—it's always been co-opted. We don't know much about the potential of group intelligence in which the individual is fully functioning.

FEAR AND SURRENDER

The idea of surrendering to the world we're in can evoke primal fear in us at the most basic element of survival. On a biological level, if I don't resist, if I don't act *into* the environment, the environment is set up to consume me. The bacteria are waiting for my flesh to make it into compost. The animal world is ready to eat me, and certainly the human world is ready to take my resources. To surrender—to give up the push-back, the aggression, the energy that pushes out into the universe and tries to create a space of safety—this looks like certain death, annihilation. A primal fear arises, and that energy, because it is primal, animates the universe with an equally primal evil—an energy that is only about destruction.

This is not the fear that you won't like me, or fear that I won't get the right job—that's everyday fear. I can do my mantra and make it through that. Most of us can manage that kind of fear one way or the other. I'm talking about a *root* fear of the mind that is so fundamental that it actually creates the very universe in which we believe we are moving. It's the basic element from which we're functioning. In that fear there's a primal evil, a force that is *only* about destruction.

This is not a force that's basically good but sometimes gets angry, sometimes loses it, sometimes makes mistakes. It's not a forgiving force, it doesn't have any compassion in it, it doesn't have any *usefulness* in it. It only has destruction.

When I begin to experience energy that drops me into primal fear what do I do with it? Do I evoke Jesus? What do you do in the face of primal evil, other than to evoke primal good?

It is clear that the force is way beyond me. I could stand up and say, "Back to Hell, you demon!" but it is just going to consume my every molecule into itself. But if I don't do anything, then the evil—because it is only about destruction— will take my body and soul and express itself through me. I would be evil.

This is worse than being killed. There's no hope that I can transcend this one—that's clear to me. It's completely evil. Jesus could help me, but I can't help myself.

In the horror movies you get the flashlight out and you go down the stairs, and of course you're always looking in the wrong direction, it's always *behind* you. Wherever you look it's coming from behind, because that's where the camera is. You have to look *to* the camera, but then when you turn, the camera circles behind!

We think, "All right, I'll go into anger and it will become power, or it'll become energy or intensity." We have a formula that says going into anger or fear is good. We'll have a little bit of awareness and turn the anger into compassion. There are systems for dealing with anger. I could breathe deeply, for example. But in the energy I'm describing you can breathe but it won't have any effect.

When we go into the energy of anger or fear, we find that we're creating a space of safety around us so that we don't actually have contact with anything. We're just pushing back all the time. If we surrender that space, then life rushes in and takes it, and the fundamental fear of being devoured by those forces arises. The energy looks like it's both outside and in-side—because it is *complete* fear. It's not part fear; it doesn't have space around it. We've dropped into the completeness of the energy.

The fear responds to this force, which is only about de-struction. You can't reach it. It's not like a bad guy comes in and you look into his eyes and you say, "Look man, you don't have to do this. I can feel you, you're okay. Just put down the gun." There's nothing to *reach*.

It is so far beyond me that everything that I can come up with is futile. Maybe I think I can go in there and whip out my sword and my shield, but the guys that do that always get vaporized in the first round. They're the pawns. So then I have to evoke the sorcerer—"Okay fine, I'll get my mag-ic staff out, got my crystal ball"...*fffp*. Those guys are the knights and bishops. Gone. Then I pull out Jesus Christ on the cross—that's the most powerful piece, the queen, right? Gone. This is the point that I realize there are no tools left, there's no capacity left.

That we are beyond all capacity to deal with it, to respond to it, to know it, to even characterize it, is something com-pletely different. This is the different dimension. The resis-tance to being consumed, which we call fear, and its projection, which we call evil, disappears.

Am I consumed, or not? This is also unknown. What it all enfolds into is unknown. I'm long gone in this story line. There isn't any actor left. There's no evil left. There's no fear left. There's nothing left.

The world that we see is a projection of ourselves, otherwise we wouldn't know the world. The only way we can know the world is by taking our knowledge and pushing it out there and characterizing it. The world we're seeing is us, what I see is what I am.

When the energy of anger perpetuates itself, is it because we know what it is? We may think that anger is not good, that it should be a different way. The fear of anger creates a space. But what if you actually don't know what it is? Would you need to create space from it, would you need to characterize it or to judge it? Isn't judgment a way of carving out space to protect yourself?

If you're stupid, then I'm not. I can see that you're stupid, so I must *not* be stupid—therefore I have space. But if you're not stupid, then the world is actually out of control. I don't have space suddenly. If you're stupid, then I can create a world in which I—the perceiver, the smart guy—can get rid of you, because you're stupid, you're dismissible. But if you're taking actions that I can't say are stupid or not, actions I can't characterize—and they confuse me because they're not the way *I* would do it—then I live in a world that's confused. I have to face the fact that I don't have any way of structuring that world, and if I can't structure the world, how do I know that I'm safe in it? Suddenly the world breaks from order—the order of "you're stupid and I'm not"—into *disorder*.

What if you make no assumptions because all the assumptions are used up? You've gone through all the ways of characterizing the energy. You are back to surrender, and it's an absolutely impossible quality because you can't *do* it, you can't make it happen. There's no button marked "surrender" in our system. There are only buttons marked "don't surrender, fight back, create space, reject, think about." Those are the buttons we have.

Living in the fear of the unknown is in a way worse than death, because what occurs in the unknown can be anything.

When a feeling, like sadness, becomes so familiar that it becomes "you," then your basic relationship to that energy is to make it known. It's sadness, and that's who you are. But when you see that the characterization isn't really accurate, you also see that there's actually a resistance to having an uncharacterized relationship to that energy.

When you characterize it, you're creating space in relation to it, you're pushing it back slightly. Surrender is giving up that space, not having any tools left to create that space, because none of them make any sense or they have all been used up. To surrender is to enfold into the quality *because* it's unknown, because you actually don't know what it is and you don't know how to respond to it. There is no movement to make. There's no space to create. It's not sadness, it's not anger, it's not evil, it's not *any* of that. It dissolves into feeling. The good/bad quality falls away.

We're always trying to characterize intensity *as* something so that it can be known, so we can know where we stand in that intensity. But it doesn't make any difference *where* we stand. If I can stand in sadness, in fear, in anger—as long as I have someplace to stand in the intensity, then I have *something*, I have a location. But intensity has no location. It can

55

express anything. It can *be* anything. *We* can be anything.

This is *worse* than death, this is being *fully alive*. To only have the non-location of life really requires that we give up trying to characterize it, give up trying to know it, trying to hold it, fix it, make it into a technology.

It requires deep feeling—not as an emotion, not as a thought—and the surrender to expression, to the movement of energy itself.

The creation of space is a way of controlling. This is what our spirituality is all about. People want to know how they can create space from energy by breathing, by paying attention. Basically, they want to know how to create numbness. It works; we can have some relative control because now we don't have to feel *anything*. We can just feel our breath going in and out and our awareness of the phenomenon.

Paying attention doesn't address creativity. What creates in a numb world in which we just have space from energy? Energy is going to move into that space, it's going to continue to move into that space, it's going to try to take that space apart. It's going to use its elbows and its teeth and its claws. We're going to be running *really really hard* to create space—breathing, breathing, awareness, awareness—because it's not true. The whole complex construction has to smash itself into one energy.

What about the pleasure or relief or peace we feel from space? I like ice cream, so I spend my days and nights at the ice cream parlor gorging on it. Does life have anything to say about that? Well, it makes me really fat and sick, and then I feel the pain that ice cream has *in* it. It's the same thing with space—I create lots of space because it's pleasurable to not feel the pain. You can create a space that is seemingly untouchable, that nothing can intrude on, where you won't feel pain. Like enlightenment, for example. The price you pay for enlightenment is that there's no vitality in the life, there's no contact. You don't feel anything.

The creation of space *is* pleasurable in the sense that it creates a feeling of safety, but that feeling of safety has insecurity and fear embedded in it. It's not really safe. There *is* no safety.

Big space has big pain waiting as the energy moves, and no matter how big your awareness is, no matter how deeply you breathe, it won't be enough to remain untouched.

LIFE IS SHIT

One could argue that life is shit—even love turns to shit. When you get what you want, at the same time you get what you don't want. You touch the most sublime space, you connect in a deep way, and then from that experience of great expansion and integration and beauty the rebound sends you crashing back into reality, which is fragmented and disconnected. Then you try to fight your way back to the sublime state again.

When we're in the sublime state, which happens somehow through grace rather than through any effort, why don't we hang out there? Why does it wear off? Why do we plunge back into the sordid nature of the divided life? Some people who claim to be enlightened masters say that they *do* hang out there, full of life, but if life is shit then they're full of shit!

My training would encourage me to let the feeling that life is shit pass through without getting involved in it. But what if, instead, you've got to go into that feeling and really feel that life is shit—go *deep* into it, get lost in it, become disconnected in it?

Going into it is getting stuck, is losing all connection—that's what the shit is. Identifying with the shit *is* the shit, where you have no hope but grace, where it looks like shit is all there is. Or can we be captured by the shit and still stay in contact with the whole at the same time?

If identification with a quality fixes that quality, but going deeply into the quality without identifying it as yourself allows dynamic movement, then that means we don't need to identify with the shit, but we can't identify with the sublime either. Are we willing to make that trade-off? When a great expansion comes, when the feeling of love comes, then that's not me either? Is freedom worth that?

What is the experience, if there's not a central reference to it? When the force isn't personified in *my* realm—it's not *me* having pain or *me* backing up from pain or *me* floating in pain—what's that energy? What's the sea without the boat floating in it, or the shores defining it?

Is the experience of bliss the dropping out of the self rather than the quality of what it has dropped out *of?* Does the self dropping out allow all kinds of energies to move without a problem—some of them being quite destructive or creative, some being quite intense, some being shitty?

Can we explore the energy taking place without the defining self in it? If you have the defining self, you are left with the question of either dropping *back* from the experience or dropping *into* the experience, but there's still a defining element that doesn't really allow the fullness of whatever the energy is. Is it possible to experience within a system, to experience whatever is taking place in a room as "the room," not as "me"? That is clearly just a bigger version of "me," but nonetheless, can we experience actuality without naming it, without identifying with it?

This is a different kind of relationship to each other, really, because there's not an *each other*, there's a systemwide energetic movement. It can't function conceptually because there isn't really a developed concept for it. The conceptual world is self-referential, so we have to abandon that as a means.

What is a relationship to energy? Is there a relationship at all? Is there any alchemical relationship or is it all just passive? Can we simultaneously occupy a space of complete surrender and acceptance of what is and a space of dynamic movement, of synthesis, of alchemy, of intention, of attention—not just passively, but actively? Can that be represented in each of us *and* collectively in the system?

Typically, in a system one person will take on the active role and others will take on the passive role. But in the breaking down of that structure we all have the opportunity to be active or passive or both. As a system, we can be active and passive individuals in a passive system—we can just show up, put in our time, and leave; *or* we can show up and create something. There's so much potential in that as a system, and the system can expand into a larger system, if we want to explore that.

Could world peace show up? Or healing? Feeding the children? What's the potential of the open space? That's the active principal of it, and of course the passive principal is the "what is"—and without that, the active principle can't happen. If you're in resistance to what is then you're just pushing against it, you're not creating.

In a system there has to be the possibility that both receptivity and activity can take place in anyone. This is quite evident in interpersonal relationship. But do we actually trust the system?

When you look at it from the individual point of view, if it's your habit to be active, you think, "Well that's what I am, I'm a transformer, that's what I do, and these people need me to be that because they're going through shit and they need *me* to help them through it." That sets up a relationship about a particular structure. But, looking at it from a system, do I trust that they have the capacity to move through it, or do I make them into people who don't have that capacity—only I have that, they don't?

In fact, what I see is that life moves through each of us. Each of us has the capacity, and this makes it a very different kind of relationship. It expands the capacity. Instead of the transformer guy helping the little people, we're *all* transformers. It *does* mean that each of us has to go through the shit, in an autonomous fashion—an autonomy that is intrinsically enfolded into the whole.

Then what's the help in that situation? It isn't helping them manage and navigate the apparent separation that they're experiencing, but rather communicating from the connection. If you're in and from the connection, then of course the other is also in and from the connection, and then they have as much capacity as you do. That's the remarkable thing.

Helping disappears in that. Helping can only be an action from an individual to an individual and not the expression of a system.

If you take the role of the helper then you're distancing yourself from the actual experience. In other words, there's something in the system that is resisting the fullness of the energetic movement, whatever that is. Now the system breaks into two parts—the person who's resisting it and needs help, and the helper. Both aspects are distancing themselves from what's actually happening.

It's about the resistance in *me* taken as an aspect of the system, but because it's the aspect that makes most sense to me—whether I'm the victim or the helper—then it has logic to it. If I see it from the whole, then I lose my role. I'm no longer the helper, no longer the transformer. Now I'm the system and the system is resisting this full contact—what do *I* need to do?

But no help is actually needed. In letting go of the role of the helper and the helped, you abandon the resistance. What you're left with is feeling, the thing that you're both trying to avoid. You've just plunged into feeling. Where's the help? There's no help needed, just deep feeling. It feels like shit or it feels like bliss—this is the description level. But if you don't describe it, where are you? If you consistently don't describe it, and your vantage is from the system, what does that relationship system become? What does a relationship system become if it doesn't describe itself to itself? What does it begin to touch? This is the transformational energy, because now it has the ability to touch a larger system.

We can and *do* fit into various roles. We have roles that might be described as being the helpers and the helped, and whatever the system needs we'll take those roles. But is there an intelligence that can live in a system without getting implanted back into an individual as a habit structure, that remains fluid and responsive to the dynamic energy?

THE LOVE OF UNCERTAINTY

Sometimes we talk about thought as if it's the enemy of energy. The sublime quality moves into the density, the pain of thought. But is it different from the sublime, or is it the same thing? If we subtract the naming of it, we'd have to say it's all energy, and then we can subtract that name too.

If there's no fragmentation, then what's creating the structure? In the energetic world, what creates the structure of thought? We may posit thought as a force outside the totality, but it's an expression of the totality, a function of the energy. Energy creates it. Thought thinks *it* creates everything. This is part of its hall-of-mirrors trick, but once you see thought as the created, then you see that thought really has a different quality.

Emotion, too, is a certain structure. Emotion has to do

with transactional feeling. You do something and I feel bad because of it. This suggests a certain quality. Thought suggests a divided world with a center and external objects. Thought and emotions are aspects; they're not the world as it is.

Without going into an ideal that you're in totality, stay with what you actually find. You may find that you can touch a systematic intelligence in your environment. You *may* even be able to touch something outside of that systematic intelligence. You may feel you can go to the whole planet, but are you going there or are you going to an ideal, a pretty picture?

Do we have the capacity to touch those primal, archetypal, universal energies? Perhaps, but those energies are also going to kick us back to whatever the conditioning is. When archetypal evil walks through the door, where do you go? Are you ready to stand in that? When primal love walks in the door, are you ready to be swallowed into it?

It's going to kick you back. It's like the experience of walking into the mountains and having a huge expansion and then the next day finding yourself crashed into your conditioning in your everyday life. Love takes you directly to what you fear—that's the expression of love. Love doesn't just leave you basking in sublime fullness, it takes you to the crud, it takes you to everything that's corrupted in your system, in your relationships, in the world. This is why love may come in the form of pain. This is why you can't recognize it. You can't recognize the thing you think you want because it comes in a form that's unrecognizable. You pray to the Goddess and she shows up as Kali and starts chopping your head off. You think, "I was asking for the Goddess, what's this?" Well that *is* the Goddess, you just don't recognize the form of it.

Only when you see that it's *all* the Goddess, *every single aspect* of it that walks through the door is life, then maybe you're ready. But this is going to be tested immediately. Because life is *going* to walk through the door. It's going to walk into your psyche, and it's going to kick your butt. Are we ready for that?

We're *not* ready if we're suggesting ideals to ourselves of things that aren't actual. If we have a cultic mindset that thinks, "We're touching all kinds of great qualities" then we only get what we expect, because it's the only thing we recognize. It's the only thing we'll let in the door. We'll expel anything else that doesn't fit in with that agreement. But if we say there is no agreement and whatever walks in the door is the Goddess, then that's a pretty vulnerable and open world. Is that true in our lives? Is it true in our relationships?

We don't have any place to stand in this vulnerability. I was telling someone that I didn't want to go into a room where I didn't know what was behind the door—the experience of a shy person—and she said you have to be ready to confront that. Okay, so I won't be shy, now I'll be an aggressive person, but I have to be ready to confront that too. Whatever role you land in, however you adjust to the reality that presents itself, that role is going to be pulled out from under you. I can't be a shy person, I can't be an aggressive person, I can't be *anything* as a habit. And there's the door. Am I a shy person or an aggressive person? I have no idea, and yet the hand moves, the door opens, and behind the door is *something*. This is the constant removal of any way of having security. When we accept the truth that there is no security, we arrive at the love of uncertainty. Love is the surrender to uncertainty, but love is also the response to that surrender in every possible form in which life shows up.

Individually, we can't deal with *any* archetype. These

energies cannot be met by the individual on any level. If you've accessed these structures as an individual, then you've accessed insanity. When we say let's invite in the energy, the energy comes in, and no individual can meet it. You can be the meditator of the century, you can be ready to die and all the rest of that. It's beyond *you*. There's no structure in the individual that can handle that movement, the play of primal energies.

We give up what we know to enter that play. The actuality is the cutting edge of what I am, and I recognize it by what I know. But I *also* know that what I know isn't it, and so then I'm constantly dropping off the edge.

Of course the challenge is that once I say I know something, it's not that. Somehow that knowing *is* the movement of the totality, but it can't be captured or described by the normal means. Somehow it's *lived*, and the exploration is how to give that expression, which mostly consists of discarding what I thought the expression was. Even in describing that, it becomes something. That description isn't really it either. But there is a movement coming from the whole.

Nothing that *I* have as an individual can know authentically, so it is somehow left to a collective knowing, which does pass through this individual and finds expression, whether passive or active.

But that expression has to move fluidly through the whole system, and the system can't be contained. It can't be just a particular group of people or system of belief. The system has to be an open system that can change and move.

DIALOGUE IS A RELATIONSHIP

Can you follow the movement in your own body and connect it to the system around you? If you're tired, lie down and take a nap. If you're angry, express it. If you need to walk out of the room you're in, then do so. Can you look at what takes place in your system and move, or must you contain yourself within the idea of who you should be?

A child has the ability to do everything in rapid succession and with little memory of what just happened. A child can be completely devastated one moment and then be laughing the next. You can ask them what they were crying about and they don't even remember, because it already moved through their system.

I was at a retreat in which we had reached a really still point that we had worked hard to get to. Then someone came who hadn't been part of the group up until then, and they brought their little kid. The irritation rippled through those adults who had achieved such a pristine space. The child, of course, was not still and was not *going* to sit still, and went into the center of the circle and started moving. Just moving moving moving moving, stomping on the floor. You could see that the child was manifesting the energy of that room that no adult would dare express.

We *talk* about letting the energy move, but *will* we let the energy move?

The child isn't sitting there thinking, "Well, can I let the energy move?" The child is simply moving. We could have shut that child down and said, "Hey, this is a special place, a retreat, this is still, shhh." And the child would learn, "Oh *that's* what you do in these places." *We've* learned that's what you do in these places—you sit up, you pay attention, you don't say anything stupid, and you talk only if you have something profound to say. Or you can take the role of the universal searcher who's confused and needs help. There are roles that we take in the spiritual construct.

We are armored bodies containing behaviors that we're supposed to be. From that we extrapolate a psychological reality, which we say we are, and we live in a disconnected mental world. Then we come to places where we *talk* about that disconnected mental world as if it exists and as if there's something to solve in it.

The body *does* exist, it's actual, and it's the place we won't go.

You won't go there because you are at a retreat and you find that you're stiff from sitting, so you guess you have to move, but if you move, everyone will look at you, and you're not supposed to move, and anyway you paid money for this thing so you're going to get every important second out of it. You're tired but you're not going to take a nap, you're not going to lie down on the floor—that's socially incorrect. You really don't like what this character is saying, but you're not just going to stand up and say, "Look, this is not true," because that would be embarrassing.

We contain all that behavior into a "spiritual person."

There is a hierarchy in the spiritual setting and it is artificial, and we're maintaining it because it allows us to hide out. If there's not a hierarchy, then it means that we're *all* responsible. Each of us, fully responsible. Do you want to be responsible for your fear and anxiety?

For a teacher to sit up in front of a group of spiritual seekers, the teacher has to have the pretense of no doubt. That's a big problem. The seekers have to have doubt to sit there, and the teacher has to have surety, and both are untrue. The fact is we cannot continue to explore within a hierarchy. I have nothing to impart and you don't have any problems to solve. We have to find a new structure if we're going to continue to explore the question. We can either make the hierarchy transparent and say, "We understand that there's a speaker and there's an audience, so at least it's out." We can agree that it's fine because it's functional. In a company, people appoint somebody as the accountant and somebody as the general manager, without making them into God. This person's good with numbers and this person's good with organization, so the company works better. It's a hierarchy, it's functional, it's transparent, everybody knows that, and it doesn't make one person better.

Post-spirituality has no position in it, and there's no accumulation of knowledge. It's not that the more time you spend in it, the better you are. There are no experts, and there's no ability to explore without *co*-exploring, without dialogue, without mutuality.

The difference is simply in that transparent or non-transparent construct. If I just walk into a gathering and I'm the speaker and we never talk about it, we never reveal it—that's not transparent. It's just embedded in the reality and we all accept it as real. But if we make it transparent, we see that it's actually *unreal*, it's just a way of organizing a mini-society for a few hours.

Are you willing to be the one who is profound in your life? Be profound and then the speaker's chair up front becomes the chair in the audience, and then we have a dialogue. The room begins to bend then. It's not set up as "audience and speaker," because there's a dialogue going on. This requires each of us to step into the dialogue fully. Once you back off and say, "I'm confused, and you've got the answer," then the dialogue is broken. All we can explore then is the hierarchy. We can explore and experience spirituality and its limitations.

Dialogue is a relationship, one that requires radical honesty. Hierarchy doesn't require anything of you. You can come, sit down in the chair, pay your money, resent paying that money or feel that you got a good deal for it, and you can basically just be passive. But in dialogue you are fully stepped into it, there's no place to hide. You *have* to go with what is true, what you feel.

What we call "relationship" is not contact. The way we construct relationship to the people in our life isn't relationship, because we're constructing it. Deconstruct that, and see what's there. It's not that there's nothing there. There's *something* there, and the question of what that something is, *is* relationship.

THE PRICE OF CONNECTION

If I say to you that if you could just let go of all your concepts then you and I could have a great relationship—the problem is *your* concepts—this is very convenient. It's a nice way to live life, always saying that it's *you*. But now I have an unfortunate collision with the fact that there's no *me* and there's no *you*. I have the radical observation that this thing I'm looking at is *me*. What do I do with "your" concepts? I'm stuck. They're not *your* concepts.

When I look at you, I am looking at my own mind. This is the beauty of life. The mind—what I am—is showing up on the screen all the time. I can say to that screen, "If you would just be better, I would be happy," but it's not a divided world. It would make just as much sense to say, "If I was happy, you would be better." We could perhaps agree that if I was happy, I wouldn't complain so much about you. But then I realize that complaining makes me happy and the fact that you won't be better allows me to complain, therefore you make me happy by making me unhappy.

This is why the whole notion of improvement is ridiculous. Where do you stand to improve? Where do you put the lever to move the universe, if it's just one thing?

How do you step "outside of" to take the position? The way *I* do it is I think, "I'm over here and you're over there and *I'm* going to improve *you*." This is breaking the world into two things. Then I notice that when I've broken the world into two things, I want to have the feeling of connection, and it's always just beyond me. The price of connection is that I see you *are* me, and I don't have the luxury of saying, "You're the problem."

Once you break the world into two things, you have endless sorrow, there's no solution to it, which of course keeps the psychiatrists and spiritual teachers quite busy. Keeps us *all* busy actually. The whole arc of changing, of improving, of getting what I want, doesn't have any meaning though. Instant liberation from the therapeutic approach to life! But that liberation means that I can't stand back from life.

It's not a subject-object world; it's just a world of energy, movement. You can't stand back from any of it.

Try to find two things anywhere outside of your mind's description. This is a hint at the human potential. The human potential is not in me improving you. The human potential is in recognizing this unitary *fact* as what I am.

THE QUANTUM PERSPECTIVE

The factual world, the physical world, is a world that simply appears out of the quantum soup, out of nothingness. Something occurs—that's it. No causality, no skill, no improvement; it just simply is. That's what we are. You cannot find causality; you cannot find the thing that causes what we are.

When the creativity begins to move, with that comes total risk. Nothing new gets created without risk, because we don't know what is being created—it's unknown. It *can't* be known or it wouldn't be creative. This is the question in each of our lives—can creativity move? Will we take the risk of creativity? Or are we so enamored with our security that we'll never take that step?

The social construct is designed to be efficient, to provide security, safety, and surety—or so it appears. The price for that safety and security is that we don't get to live. But life is trying to move through each of us, and life's not going to be stopped.

What's the evidence that we're alive? Feel the energy. Do you see its manifestation? Where is it manifesting?

If you take away the thinking, the conceptualization, time, then you have energy, but no description, no past and no future. Find movement. Look into the relationship of stillness and movement. Are they the same, are they different, does one come from the other?

When you start to *tell* about your experience, this is the creation of time, and in time you have to have a location, so you have to step outside the experience, and now you have a description. This is the realm of mind. Without stepping back from it and describing, there's just the energy—still and moving.

Here's the very subtle trap of the non-dual perspective— we see that it's all one, therefore everything's fine, it looks good. Once I say that to myself enough times I'm like Ramana, and that's really great. But this is the constructed space again—the stepping back. What actually takes place? I say it's all one, but what happens in me is agitation about, or movement through, what is—an active dynamic expressing in the passive stillness. There is a creative movement going on, and to deny that is to get stuck in the masculine quality, the Shiva quality. Shiva's one part of it and Shakti's the other part. It's perfect, it's all still, it's all the way it is, *and* Shakti is dancing. Are *we?* Or are we afraid of the dance, afraid of the feminine, afraid of the movement of life, the directionality of consciousness? It's still and it's moving; it's not just stillness and it's not just movement. *Just* movement is neurotic, and just stillness is the inability to move. It's all perfect *and* it's also dynamic and changing.

If we look back, there's nothing to see, really. It is perfect because it is what took place, but all we can see is our memory of it anyway, a memory entirely constructed. What moves from this moment? Not in time—you have to step out of the past-present-future, the linear Newtonian physical perspective, into a quantum physical perspective. The quantum physical reality is that anything is possible in this moment. What is it that creates where anything is possible? And what is created? This is the investigation.

GOING DEEPER INTO OUR OWN LIFE

Y ou are both the big cosmic consciousness and the individuated consciousness. If you're just in the big space and don't attend to the individuated consciousness, then you're a mad woman running around with a shopping cart on the streets. You have to take care of, and be concerned with, all aspects of life, which include what *you* are. The undulation between these two aspects has a function.

We came out of the desert, we got resurrected, and we've had the merger with Godhead, and then we walk back into the marketplace. When you slam back into your own being, there's all your conditioning. Why would the expanded space want to be expanded all the time? From *our* personal perspective, it feels good and peaceful and we don't have to deal with the challenges of our conditioning, but why would the expanded space, the ineffable whole, want to be in the midst of our personal mess?

We don't know what totality wants, but it does seem that it moves from the expanded space *into* this mess called our life, into "me," rather than the other way around. We'd never be able to get there. We can't take our mess into the expanded space because we'd just have an expanded mess. When you step out of the grasping and look at what grasping is trying to produce, it's an absurdity. As a person, I can grasp to fulfill my desires, but how does the universe try to get more than everything? The direction does seem to be the engagement of the messiness by the whole.

We think that because we exist, there must be a point, but we're really not sure. All we've done so far is to throw away the points of reference that we thought we had, and notice something about the movement of wholeness into the conditioning, and back out and in again. There's an undulation or movement, a wave-like vibrational quality, that occurs constantly, but not in time, and not just in special spiritual places where there's a certain dynamic set up. There's a change in intensification, and the undulations—the wavelengths, the spaces between the changes—are variable.

When the body contracts in fear, we feel that in the stomach, and when we're in love, we feel that in the heart. These qualities within the body system aren't exactly emotions and aren't exactly thoughts, but they have emotions and thoughts attached to them. When I'm in my heart I have the thought, "I love this person," and I have the feeling of wellbeing.

We think of our experiences as if they're located in our bodies, but perhaps they're not. Could we read the newspaper and change world events by taking in the world? Could my heart be *the* heart, my mind *the* mind?

Is it possible that the ineffable whole knows what it's doing when it comes into *my* mind, the mess of my mind, the mess of my conditioning? What if there's no time and no space, and qualities appear to be occurring in my system, my mind, my conditioning, my mess, but it isn't actually mine, isn't in time or space? It's *the* mess; the ineffable whole is plunging into *the* mess.

We would like to experience that transformative energy is hitting our lives and we are fully aware that we are timeless, spaceless human beings who are in fact the metaphoric, holographic representation of the universe. But that isn't what we actually experience.

We contract into our individual mess and lose the perspective that our individual mess is *the* mess and that in fact we are the point of transformation of the universe, and that we are the world mother transforming, birthing the new world. Why do we lose that perspective?

When we find ourselves contracted into the personal space, we might ask, why is intelligence revisiting that place over and over and over again? We push the contraction and fear away and think, "I shouldn't do that." If it's intelligence and it keeps coming back to that place, maybe we should go into that place with intelligence. Maybe it's not really contraction into some individual place, maybe it's still transformative. It's just that we've interpreted that place as bad, as not a transformative place, so we've resisted the contracted space or reacted to it in a certain way as a pattern, rather than fully embracing it as the movement of intelligence, rather than going deeper into our own life.

If we haven't found anything that isn't intelligent, that is not an expression of the ineffable whole moving through the world of apparent form, then we also have to bring this perception into the actual experience of our life. This is where the rubber hits the road. When we contract into the world of individuated messiness—the *appearance* of that—can we see the intelligence in it, release into it, from it, through it, and discover some other quality going on? Or is the world of appearance so concrete for us that it *is* the world, and all the rest is just abstraction? That's the challenge—that the world of intelligence *is* our world, that we *are* living that, that it is real for us.

VIRTUAL
REALITY

Life doesn't have anything to do with what *we* want. It doesn't have anything to do with our description, our conditioning, our direction. It's not that it's doing what it wants, because there's no "it" that wants. Life just is. It's tremendously dynamic and yet it does not move from location to location. It doesn't move in time—doesn't move in any way that we can think about or describe. If we attend to what is actual in our life, we'll see that our life has absolutely nothing to do with our description, nothing to do with the way we *think* about what's happening. We are not in control of our life or anything else, but we live as if we have that capacity. We struggle to have control, to define life, to direct it, to own it.

What is the expression of feeling in us? What is the restriction of it? Can we let it express itself? What's actually moving, and will we let it move?

We constantly take energy into the mind, into a description, over and over again. The mind has patterning that we identify as control. It's mechanical, habitual, chronic, so we say that's predictable and I control it. But if you don't move energy into your mind and disconnect yourself from your own body, your own life, your own presence, what happens?

You have to find out by doing it, by not resisting, by not taking all that energy constantly into the mental area. This means the philosopher may have to move around. It means their stoicism, their ability to control energy by sitting still and making precise descriptions of it, is actually an avoidance. Pretty much everything we do is an avoidance. Our whole life is a conversion of moving energy into something that *appears* to be in our control, *appears* to be stable. We try to push it into certain kinds of relationships, certain kinds of activities, things that we know about, things that are not risky. But there are all kinds of energetic movements that are not expressing. Where do they go? What happens to a body that doesn't express itself, that doesn't allow expression, that wants to move, but is restricted from moving, that wants to call out or cry out and doesn't?

Pain, pain, and pain, in all forms. Pain in the outer forms— the breakdown of relationships, the breakdown of finances, the breakdown of health. And in the inner world, calcification or hardening of the space. This *looks* like control, like "I've got something here" in the inner space. "I found something, I know something, I am somebody." That's what it looks like, but it's actually resistance to the movement, which is alive, creative, and has all the human potential in it.

This energetic movement destroys what's false in relationships. In that destruction it deepens the actual relationship, because the actual relationship is a fact, not an idea. It destroys the falseness of activity that is not whole.

It is both the destruction of what's false and the creation of something whole, because that's what it is—it is alive, it is whole. Resistance to that movement is pain, pain, and pain. There's absolutely no movement to the resistance. It's the illusion of time and process, the spirituality of getting better.

We tend to try to modify our conflict, to relieve the absolute pressure, the absolute pain of relationship conflict, but this attempt to fix it actually makes it more difficult. If you and I work out our communication with each other so that we feel better about each other, this is actually a worse condition than being in total conflict, because in total conflict we're right in contact with something extremely vital. But in our self-improvement, we're replacing that uncomfortable contact with an ideal that suggests we're getting better, when all we're doing is thinking we're getting better.

I'd rather be in contact with the actual resistance, the pain of it, and the possibility of that pain releasing because it's too much. I would prefer to be flattened by my own resistance. To actually feel what that is. But that's the movement of feeling again, isn't it? And that moving energy will rip apart anything that is not true, that is not the expression of that movement.

The mentalized world that resists energy doesn't have substantial existence. It's a virtual world where we hide, and the hiding, the virtual world, and the "we" that hide there are all without substance. It's like a computer game where all the senses are somehow engaged, as if we're walking down the street, as if a monster jumps out, as if we have the ray gun. This has all the qualities of actuality, but in fact it's just a trick of the senses. The aggregation of those senses would suggest that I live in separation, that I know something, that I am something.

You can't find that world in feeling—it doesn't exist in that form at all. You find something that is like that—thinking takes place in feeling, feeling expresses itself through thinking, but there's no separate world in that feeling. There's a separate world seamlessly connected to a whole world. What you find in actual life is relationship, movement of energy, which means that all that separation you build from the aggregation of the senses *isn't*.

Do I want to see that I am not? Does the aggregation want to see that it is not? Certainly not. In that friction we find the quality of sublime confusion. It's the *dis*organization of what we *think* we are and, at the same time, a sublime quality of connection with feeling. It's destruction and creation at the same time.

Feeling is not in the virtual world because it's not describable. It can't be taken into the conceptual world. When we try to do that, we get philosophy and spirituality.

ANGER

What is anger? How does it describe the universe? What does the universe look like from anger? Why does it persist? Is it possible it's not an experience or even an energy, but an entire relationship to life? If someone brought to my attention the possibility that my fundamental relationship to life is anger, it really would really piss me off!

How would I know if anger—the desire to move something out of my way if it's an obstacle—characterized my entire relationship to the world around me? As long as something's aligned with me, cool, no problem. But if it's in my way, I'll push it out of the way, and do so with artful means—insight, perception, even love. Basically, the relationship to life is "in my way." If that is the relationship, how can I even see that? It's so embedded.

Let's bury all assumptions in the actual flow of life. Let's make it clever by saying that there is no me, there is only the perception of what is, and everything in the way of that is resistance. That's a clever version of me.

In my world, *you're* the resistance and *I'm* the perceiver. There's no me here, I'm clear on that, you think you're a "me" so you're in the way.

This is impenetrable logic. If I set my life up so that basically you have to come to me, there's a subtle power structure there. I don't leave my house except for special events, retreats, dialogues. How would I see it in that world? There's no me, so I can't be getting angry—it's just anger happening.

Understand that when I require that things be a certain way, this is not a psychological certain way, this is a deeply mystical certain way. But we're certainly still in a world where there's something that irritates us. So we could say it's a transformational world, but let's say it's moving from form to form. This form moving to that form is still a kind of irritation. So I say I'm in a transformational space, and anyone who touches my life is going to be transformed. That sounds very angry doesn't it?

In the world where change just happens, what characterizes that world? Change, only change. We can say we experience change as energy, but we don't actually experience change. That's a gap. Change is from this form to that form. You can describe the forms but not the gap, so you experience something for which we're using the word *energy*. Am I that energy, am I observing that energy, are you that energy? Where does energy exist in my world?

If we experience energy as anger, that experience is in a personalized form, it's not just impersonal. The nature of experience is that something characterizes it, this is the personal. Impersonally, you can say it doesn't have any quality at all.

Here's the subtle thing—when I say *I* am in the impersonal energy, I'm characterizing it, and that characterization

is then a broad relationship to life. Otherwise there's no relationship to life, there's no experience, there's just the thing
we're calling change, which doesn't have any characteristic at
all. There *is* relationship to life, we all have it, and my question is what is it? Is it possible that my relationship to life
is to be angry? I'm not saying it's bad. Maybe this is what a
transformational life is—pissed off at life as it is, and wanting to kick it into some new form. That's a certain kind of
energy.

Is our purpose to *transcend* the anger or is it to *realize* the
anger? Does this anger energy need transmuting? We can really only understand the quality of being angry in terms of
it happening to *me*, something happening that I don't like—
this is where the personal comes in. I don't like you, I don't
like the way you look at me, therefore I'm enraged.

The personal aspect of it is a way of not being touched
by anything, it's a safe place. If I can overpower you, push
you out of the way, I'll never be touched. Is this quality personal? If you and I sit together, then that space becomes em-
powered, hot, angry—we're using that word but it's really
not anger—it becomes intense. And something moves. That's
a relationship to life and that is what I am basically. Most
fundamentally, I'm not anything, nothing there, there's just
change, which has no characteristic at all. But wherever I can
get to what I am, it has that quality. What happens when you
are that? It doesn't just work externally, but also in the life
within. So is this true, or is it basically a self-serving description of a person who's irritated but wants to have a feeling of
transformation or enlightenment in their life?

Life's going to kick your ass. Do you really want that? I
don't. This is why we hide out in the personal. But if you and
I allow each other in, it still may be transformational. We can

knock down all the barriers, and there still may be something there that we would interpret as personal anger, but it's impersonal intensity, which burns, which is white rage. It's hot; it starts to burn through all the structures of our resistance to each other.

An Indifferent Universe?

If I live in a timeless place, form is going to produce resistance. Every kind of structure is going to form resistance to that timeless place, because energy always disintegrates form. All form can do is react, and that reaction is what the *experience* of anger is. But then the broader question is, why is the suggestion that anger is my relationship to life coming in at all? Why is life presenting that suggestion to me? That suggestion has to become a deeper question than my response. I have to question my response to that, and see if even that relationship of timelessness and form is an expression of anger, an expression of changing what is. This is a very interesting question about alchemy: Does the force of change have intelligence when it transmutes the condition from one thing to another, to a deeper level of integration? For me, that goes to the ambivalence of even engaging in a dialogue like this. The only reason I would do that is for transformation, but now I have to question even the intelligence of transformation.

The worldview in which things just happen leaves out the possibility that the universe moves through individuals. So it moves through me and I can change you. From my experience, which is the only place I can get to it from, I have the experience that I can change people. I change you. The experience is that there's a perception of the psychic structure, and a movement of energy shifts that structure into a more integrated place. If I don't refer to my experience, what's the actuality? Does change just happen, in which case there's no need for me to show up anyplace in particular? Or is change happening because of a particular dynamic, which is taking place *because* we show up with intention?

An aspect of life is indifferent. But indifference would indicate an unchanging quality, and clearly there are energetic changes and directional movements one can see. On a broad scale, there's a movement or a concentration of a certain quality that's not indifference.

If it's an indifferent universe, then change is just happening, and it doesn't really matter whether we do anything in particular or not. Why would it? Yet we do engage with each other for some reason that indicates something that is not indifferent. I don't come to a dialogue indifferently; I come with a deep intention. But I don't know that anyone else will walk through the door or what condition they will come in. That doesn't look indifferent to me.

Are we so unavailable to simply move, to allow movement to take place, whatever it is?

Can't we move the energy of the dialogue from a stuck place, which is like a theoretical ping-pong match, into something that is alive, where energy is moving and transforming? Isn't there an inertia in bringing it back constantly to theory or idea? This brings us back to the question of what the energy is. If the energy shows up as boredom and agitation and wanting to push into the space to make it open up and come alive—to confront—is that intelligent?

To put it another way, if we're interested in anger, why aren't we angry? It's like reading a book on what a frog looks like. Why not just find a frog? The energy is trying to come up, but what are we doing with it? Everybody is irritated by somebody else in *some* way. So what's the relationship to that energy?

I trust the feeling to push it. Is that anger, non-acceptance? It is more holistic than that. That's what the energy is producing in me. I'm not reacting to any particular person in this system, I'm reacting to the system itself—that we came together for a transformational relationship and it's turned into a chat session. Some people feel that you just let it find its own expression, but what moves through *me* is to make it transformational. It's not an expectation, it's what is present for me, an intensification. I feel the whole thing in my body, so I don't feel outside of the movement of this group. It's actually in me; it *is* me.

We have the idea that a heated exchange is a problem and therefore we shouldn't go there. This is how the love of the energy takes you wherever it goes, and sometimes it goes into that heat, but it doesn't associate with any narrative.

The dynamic of pushing is that there's a contact happening somewhere that isn't embodying, isn't coming into the form of a relationship. The energy is trying to embody, to express through form, and unless it does, it's going to be felt as a transforming energy. When both parties are in the energy, it's in the body, in the system, and now something creative can happen.

Pain is the resistance to the movement within you. It's not external, it's not "me" pushing "you." It's your own energy, your own depth trying to emerge.

The only way for you to deliver the message that the energy is trying to embody is to show up. You can't do that from a hidden place. Your message can reach the person you're in relationship with only by the full energy coming through your form and touching that person. Then pushing is irrelevant at that point. Then there's something very creative. That's really what this is about; it's not even about transformation. Transformation is just the opening up to the full energy so it can move completely through form, and then it creates something, or maybe it just *is* creation.

Are we here to show up and discover creativity or are we here to theoretically talk about possible resistances and the possible solutions so that we *don't* actually have to step into the co-creative, co-responsible space?

I don't want to push people around out of some idea of transformation. I would like to see what love creates in relationship. That's what my heart is expressing. That creates intensity, which we can talk about as anger because that's how we know it culturally or psychologically. I want to bring that out and into every relationship. Those relationships that do not have it will react, and those that do will somehow stay. Energy begins to somehow manifest in those relationships.

The expression of this intense energy comes through each of us. That's the demand of the space—it's not coming through *a* person to *another* person. There's no receiver, no transmitter. There's the energy as it's embodied here.

Discomfort is an aspect of it, but all the sublime qualities are as well. This is the point—the intense energy has to move through everything, and if I'm with that energy then I have to go with it, through everything. This means my heavens and my hells, facing the person in deep reaction to me *and* facing the person in deep love with me. (I'm not sure which is heaven and which is hell, by the way.) But going through the whole show. Collectively, that's a remarkable thing if that can happen, in relationship.

The expression is not me, this collection of body-mind psychology interpreting the expression of intensity and then thinking, "This situation needs to be pushed, so I will tap into the intensity and push it." That is like being in a boat in the ocean and thinking, "I'm going to make the ocean go this direction because the boat has to go this way." That's not going to happen.

This intensity is not something that I turn off or turn on, but is just existent. The expression can take the form of passivity or non-involvement or non-interference, or it can take the form of strong interference.

DO YOU EXIST?

Can you prove your existence?

If you're sitting in a chair, are you aware of your leg touching the chair? Are you aware of the slight tension in your shoulders? Where is that awareness located?

When you're aware of your leg against the chair, is your whole world just "leg," just the sensation and the awareness of the sensation as the same thing, collapsed into this one place, and that's it? I'm suggesting that where you are isn't just your leg, but the whole interactive space you're in—that you are actually in a very complex location, that's where you actually live. The idea of you and me is within that complex everything. You've become over-identified with *you*—not that we shouldn't be identified at all. If you cut your toe, that identification is intelligent, because you can then patch up the cut toe.

Over-identification is the obsession with this particular location, forgetting the whole interactive place. If you remember the interactive environment, this energetic world, and you ask yourself, "Am I afraid of death?" what does that even mean in reference to the energetic world?

A frog has three things on which it focuses its visual perception. A frog's brain is largely set up to measure the level horizon of the pond for orientation, to relate to small objects that are moving quickly like insects, and to large objects that are moving slowly, like cranes that will eat it. Its whole world is basically getting food, surviving the crane, and finding out where the pond is, that's it. It doesn't have psychological fear of death; it doesn't have self awareness.

Where do you experience yourself? If your world is contracted to this self and that's it, then you're living a frog's life, and in the frog's life, the concerns are the fly and the crane. In the life of the self, the concern is the survival of the self and the motivator is the fear of death. But I don't think this is where you actually live. We live in an energetic reality. If this body dies, I'm still living in an energetic reality—not in this form, but in the energy as it forms again.

The function of the body and the self does not contradict this. The biological imperative of the body is to live, and the so-called fear of death or the response to try to live is just a natural part of the biological machinery. Our actuality is not the body *or* something else, it's the body *and* something else. The something else in relation to the body is a very interesting matter to explore.

The biological imperative for the silverback ape is that when the dominant male wins the fight for the female, he will kill all the existing offspring of other males. So obviously something else is also happening for humans. There's something connecting us in a way that is not simple biology.

But we also have a psychological identification with the self that transforms worry about the death of the body into worry about what could happen after the death of the body. Will we be in everlasting life, or are we reincarnated, or will we be nothing but energy?

If you look at what you are now, you're not just a body. To ask whether there will be everlasting life or whether this mind or this self will remain, disregards everything else that you already are. That question of death can be asked only from the contracted state; it has no meaning from the whole.

NOTHING IS REQUIRED

We come to a talk and we think, "Maybe tonight will be like last time," and if we're coming for the first time, then we think, "This might be something I would like." Usually we don't go to places we don't think we'll like. So we come to this place and then something happens that is not like what we expected, and we begin to construct an experience. This construction of an experience is the creation of the self—the subject and a world of objects—and that experience helps us understand what's taking place. Even in the structure of our brain, when we take an action or move our hand, our brain suggests to itself what that movement will feel like. If it feels like *other* than what it expects, the brain focuses attention on that movement. If it feels like something completely unexpected, the brain suggests to itself that this is something *other*—something has come in to its environment and impacted it.

This is why a chair is a chair and not *me*—because when I move my hand, it feels the way I expect it will. This is wired into us; this is how we experience the world. I come to this place, something happens, I have to wrap it into an experience, and that experience is now my understanding. Once I have that understanding, I'm okay. It doesn't matter anymore whether I like it. I thought I would like it, but now that I'm here, it's okay if I don't like it, because I have a location now. But what we're creating in *this* space is something that we cannot quite create an experience from.

What if we do not experience what's taking place here? Is that creative? Experience, remember, is forming what we *don't* know into what we *do* know. It is a biological imperative, which worked very well when we lived in the jungle. That biological imperative doesn't work very well in the contemporary world, though, because now *my* experience as a Muslim conflicts with *your* experience as a Christian. These experiences are in conflict because we've taken experience from the physiological world into the psychological world. The psychological world appears to us to be just as substantial as the physical. Where before I would die fighting the tiger, now I'll die fighting someone who doesn't agree with my beliefs—beliefs that exist only in concept.

So the question of whether we can live without continuous referencing of experience, whether we can be creative, is a fundamental question. It might answer all questions, because all questions reside in the construction of reality and the search for knowledge. The fact is that you can't know anything; all your knowledge can be deconstructed.

It is easy enough to distinguish between the physiological construction of experience and the psychological one. To accept the physiological construction is useful, but the psychological is not so useful.

You can create an imaginary world of psychological problems, but something's still happening that's not imaginary. The movement of life takes place with or without our courage or effort. Nothing is needed for that which is not imaginary to take place, but we have to stop the pretense of the roles we take on and attend to the movement of energy to recognize that.

Nothing is really required. The trick of the imaginary world is that it suggests to us requirements that we can never fulfill.

LOOKING IN THE WRONG PLACE

 Silence is another way of saying "no experience," and if we don't make anything out of silence, you would imagine that there would be nothing, that silence without doing anything would be the end of the universe. But it's interesting that when we do nothing with silence, there's still something. That something is the mystery. It's the energy of life. It's not something I'm doing or you're doing. You can live in that energy or you can create concepts from it. You can make the silence something special, something you can teach people about, you can declare yourself enlightened, or you can try to get back to it because you've lost it. You can be burdened by the fact that the silence is starting to slip away. You can fill that nothing up with all kinds of thoughts and ideas.

But still the energy is moving—*with* those ideas or without them. The question I am trying to bring forward is about energy, not my ideas or your ideas about it, but the energy as it moves, as it creates the qualities present now.

The problem with "new" is that we don't know how to get to it. We know how to get to what *was* new, but what was new last week is not what's new this week. When we try to get to new this week we're actually getting to old—last week's new. This is how we're structured. And when we get to what we *thought* was new, what's new about that is that we don't have the same experience.

So we go out on our first date together—everything is new. I've never talked to you before, I don't really know what you're like, and here we are spending time together, and it's enjoyable, and I think, "I want to have that experience again." I'm going to ask you out again. So now we go on a second date, and it's not really the same as the as the first date. I get really worried about this but I'm going to try it *again*, so I ask you out on a third date.

So, you see it is actually new—the new of the third is that it's not the new of the first date. But we don't see that new, because we're looking for the old new. Life is *always* new, but we're looking for the *old*. This is very important in relationship, because in relationship we're always looking for new. This is the ruin of so many relationships. New is always there—even in an old, old, old relationship it's always new, but we just can't recognize it. We can solve the divorce problem here!

We can't recognize it because where we look for it is in the old. We look for it in the wrong place, because if we look for it in the right place, we lose our sense of location. We're located in what we know, and in what we *don't* know we have no location. This is why we're always interpreting the new into the old. We cannot come to something and *not* know what's going on. This is the interesting thing about the new—you cannot know it. So imagine, you're in relationship to the husband or wife whom you've been with for ten years, and if you looked at them and actually recognized them, you could never *know* that person. That person is *always* new. We would always be in love.

Fixing the Energy

What happens when we stop trying to improve? Can we be just as we are? What happens when I try to be as I am? I find that this "as I am" doesn't have a clear definition, so I lose the sense of self, because my location is defined by the voice of constant self-correction.

We're never smart enough, we're never polite enough, we're never good enough. And now we're not spiritual enough, we're not enlightened enough, and we're definitely not silent enough. The voice of correction that comes from within and without presses us into location. Without that voice of correction we are simply what we are, and that can be anything. Anything is not anything *good*—anything is *anything*. Now we have to face the possibility of the shadow, the expression of what we know and what we don't know, and ultimately the question of good and evil. When there is no correction, then anything can be. Now watch the fear arise.

If what I am is completely free, if anything can express, then anything is possible—including the most horrible things. Do we still want that freedom?

We think we need to "let go," but the mechanism of letting go is the same mechanism as the judger. This is a kind of correction—that you should let go. There is absolutely nothing you can do in this realm. You feel the pressure of fear and that's it. There's no escape. There's no correction to that fear. See how you distort that fear in the act of correcting it. Without the correction, fear is not fear, it's energy. The qualities of that energy are dynamic.

We're so busy fixing the energy that we never actually go into it. This thing we call fear is really a way of trying to control the energetic movement of life, and now fear wants to fix itself. So we struggle with our fear and still it's the struggle of correction.

We can also see that we're experiencing something besides the personal energy. The interpretation is always that of a subjective, personal story. But without the interpretation or the personal story it is something *im*personal. It's not about you at all. That's *really* scary. Now your consciousness is bigger than anything you know about. Now you're really in the unknown. This is what the energetic movement really is— it's unknown. It's known to us only by its manifestation, but it's not known to us in any way that we can control. The generation of the self is an attempt to control the energy. This is absolutely ridiculous, because the energy is actually expressing itself as the very quality with which we struggle.

You don't have to do anything. Really. You don't have to do *anything* at all. Is this clear? If you sit in rooms like this as many times as I do, you'll see that often none of us really knows what we're talking about, but we continue talking, and on an energetic level something is coming together. So it's actually a brilliant contribution to this room to not know what's going on, and to be brave enough to say, "I have no idea what you're talking about." This is a room with no wrong answers.

Yesterday we were sitting like this all through the day, and one of the children started to get restless. I could either say to him, "You need to go into the no-mind," or I could say, "There's a nice cathedral, why don't you walk aaaalllll the way there." Then he walked and calmed down and became relaxed. The body may need to move. You say no-mind to the body and the body says I don't care about the mind, I care about the body. If you're agitated and you demand of yourself to be able to switch into no-mind, you're going to fail. Then you're going to come to rooms like this to get the answer to your dilemma.

The answer is really simple. If you do nothing, the body will express itself. If you stop correcting yourself, your body knows what to do. If you're sitting here today and your body starts to feel like it wants to move, could you stop correcting it, and move instead of sitting here as if you're quiet? That would be a very honest interaction and your body would feel good. You can live like that. I invite everyone here to do the same—if you feel like moving, move. This is definitely not a special religious place. You don't have to be respectful, there's no protocol. If you feel tired there are mats to sleep on, if you feel energetic move around, and if you feel like sitting still then sit still.

See how you correct yourself so that you only do what is okay in this social context. Well now I'm saying the social context here is to express the feeling, the energetic movement. There is the possibility that we can live like that, and that life has its own intelligence.

We'll find out. This is an experiment. You see, we don't know. It's much more sellable to say that *if* you follow the energy, intelligence will come from that. This is unfortunately not true. What *is* true is that if you follow the energy you'll find out. And there's a possibility that energetic organization *is* intelligence, but we can't know that until it manifests. So unfortunately there's no promise.

The energy is not in form, the energy creates form. So you're *in* the energy, but you're looking at the form, the manifestation.

We cling to the forms of the past and we're looking for those forms now. This is like wanting to have more hair because I remember that when I had more hair, I had more fun. So I think that more hair would solve my problem, but it's not in the hair. I can have more fun *now*. So go to the energy now, and see what's there.

If you stop containing the energy, it will express itself. It will move your mind and body into different places. If it moves we don't know that we will have a location in that movement. I know who I am when I have all this bundled up and kept together, but I don't know who I am if the energy is just moving. The problem with keeping it all contained is that I don't feel alive, I don't feel in this flow, in this connection. This is the real moving in life—the draw of life itself, always pushing, always pushing. This constructed self is pushing back, trying to keep it all contained, and at some point we begin to feel the tension in that. This is an existential point in the life—"Do I trust that energetic movement wherever it's going to go, or do I stay with this tremendous effort to try and keep it contained?"

You don't have any choice. Let it go.

RESISTANCE

It seems to me that the energy of life does not share our morality. The actuality is without morality. Life doesn't make a distinction between birth and death. When the tsunami came in Asia, some quarter of a million people died. In that same day a quarter of a million people were born around the world. We can look at that and say we don't know what life is doing, but life is clearly creating death and life at the same time.

There is a movement in science to prolong life essentially endlessly. In the laboratory they have altered the genetic part that affects aging, which suggests the possibility that human beings won't die. How would we deal with that? Can you even make sense of a life where there's no death? It sounds good at first, but then you realize that the earth would just fill up with people. There isn't really creation without destruction.

War and violence are in me. I'd like it to be someplace else—Iraq or George Bush—but I find that violence is in me. What happens when I see that world of death and destruction as me? Do you find that in you?

We like to think of the universe as somehow a good place, but it doesn't seem that the energy cares about our "good." I found it very disturbing to face that this energetic universe is not conditioned by what I think is good. Then the question comes, do I go with my sense of good or with this energy, into the unknown? This is a very unsettling area for most of us.

My decision would always be to go with me, my ideas. I will always resist the energy, and the energy will always smash me, and likely the same with you. I will never go into the unknown willingly. But we're all getting kicked into the unknown all the time. This exploration is about the struggle to hold on to what I know while being pushed into the unknown. We begin to see that this is the direction of the energy, it's pushing us *all* into the unknown all the time. The resistance looks terrible. The actual creative movement is beautiful.

You can only approach the energy in a negative way, by discarding every idea, every image, every notion. Everything you can find out you have to throw away, you have to continuously hold the question. But in the end you have to throw away the negation. That's the point of creation. For us philosopher men it's very easy to do the negation. We can take apart everything, but the risk of creation is usually where we falter. Holding the question is not the life of paralysis.

You can see the male-female energy here, the yin-yang. The negation is the male energy and the creation is the female energy. But the real negation is the silence. Even madness can't stand up to that.

YOU CAN'T MASTER LIFE

The power of silence brings you what's important with great intensity. Then we construct something in the face of that and think, "I don't want it, it's too much." But this is like facing your own death. You will have to face it sometime, and nobody can help you.

When these strong qualities appear, the tendency is to go away from them. But you can actually go into them and find out about them.

It's an energetic movement, so when you discover "now," it's lost. That present is the past. The energy that appears next could be completely different or it could be the same. It's not predicted by what you just went through. This is why there are no masters—anybody who claims to be a spiritual master is missing the point. You can't master life, you can't master the energy. In the next moment, it's completely new—just as difficult, just as challenging. There's just as much resistance. I'd *like* to tell you it gets easier, but it doesn't. We would love to know how to do it so that it gets easier—"Okay, I know how to do that; when it comes, I'll do this and it's good..."

It's always impossible. We're always up against the edge of our understanding. We always have to step through our own resistance into the unknown. And we're always going to be unwilling to do that. We get kicked into the unknown. So if you ever feel like you have it figured out and you can move with your energy really easily, that's not it. Even if you could move really easily with all the energy moving through your system, then you'll sit next to someone and you've got *his* energy now. You're connected to this one, to this one, to this one. And *those* energies are not moving. So finally we get this room going, it's moving—and then we step out into the street. The energetic systems are always up against resistance because of the psychic structure that we have.

How did we get to be like this?

You can see how the structure of resistance to energy becomes a location. Something moves, and I see, "Oh, this is how you do it." Now I have a location in relation to that energy. Now every time that energy comes I use this process to do whatever it is that I do. And I conduct workshops on this. Now I have the Energy Moving System. It's a culture now. This is how this psychic structure builds around the energy and tries to frame everything into the known. The world that we inhabit is a very very complex, intricate, woven, psychic structure around the energetic movement. The energy is pushing that structure into the unknown, and the structure is trying to hold itself together.

If you look inside and outside, you see that this resistance has some relationship to the energetic movement. If you had no resistance, just energetic movement, you'd have nothing—there'd be no *thing* there. There's no distinction, no manifest universe, so the resistance and the energy together create everything we see in the universe.

Now there's a very interesting question that I don't know whether we have the capacity to address, which is about the nature of creation and resistance and what it produces. The big problem is that what we can function in is causal—first this, and then that. But the manifestation seems to occur without causation. How do you transform something that has nothing before it and nothing after it?

We address the energy from the resistance, rather than addressing the energy from the energy. Can human beings *live* in this energy? We know we can live in the resistance— this is where we are now. This is the question of human consciousness, and it does look like madness. Maybe this is divine madness, or maybe this is psychiatric madness, but to really go into this question you have to say you don't know. It would not be surprising if there were a couple of guys in white coats in here trying to give us our medicines. Because when you start to delve into a formless energetic universe, and there is no location, there's no time, and there's no meaning (because without before and after there isn't time or meaning, and there's no location because there's nothing referencing that), then what is it?

It looks like nothing, and yet there's something. This is the mystery, and in a way everyone in this room is part of that experiment, whether you like it or not. It's not an area where a master or a brilliant person or a person of knowledge can function. It's actually a place where only the common person can function. If you think you know something, you're not in the exploration, you're somewhere else. The willingness to not know anything, and to stay in that field of not knowing, is very fragile.

You think resistance is bad and you think you shouldn't have it. You think there's an ideal state of no resistance. This is still the attempt to improve yourself. What you find when you go inside *is* resistance. Then you look at the front of the satsang room and there's some guy who says—in words or in symbols—that there is no resistance in *this* one. Or you read in a book that there's something called enlightenment, which must mean no resistance. You think, "Okay, I'm going to get to that place of no resistance," but every time you check in, you find resistance. So you try harder and harder.

Resistance is what creates the universe. If you find no resistance, you find nothing.

You *do* have resistance, and the idea that you could *not* have resistance is an idea. If one day you wake up and you find absolutely no resistance, you will also find absolutely nothing. Without resistance there's nothing defining the energy. The resistance is the edge of your capacity and the energy is pushing you past that edge. Are you feeling resistance to what I'm saying? That resistance is defining this relationship—it makes a distinction between you and me. That's a universe—if there's no resistance, then there's no universe, there's a collapse of you and me.

Look at what occurs in your life not as "it should be different," but rather as "what is it?" and you will see the movement of pushing against the energy and then the release of that. The pushing against this energy is what we call thought. What thought is, is what we see. Without resistance there's just energy—no thought, silence, and nothing there.

┬Freedom

When we ask ourselves what's next in our spirituality, we can only ask that seriously if we're willing to leave behind everything that has happened up to this moment. If we require a reference to what we know, then we will miss what's next. There is the past, there is what's next, and unfortunately there is no now. I know that we have learned a lot about the power of now in the past few years, but the now that we learned about is the past. If we dwell on that present, we are living in the past, which is stale, and not alive.

So I wonder if you can give up the present moment, and give up all the efforts you have made to be in the present moment—all those hours of seminars, all those hours of meditation, all the pressure to be "present"—when the mind is always calling us to be in the past or in the future. The now is a concept. All concepts are of the mind, and the mind by its nature is a reflection of the past. If you want to know where you've been, you can look to the mind. This may tell you some little bit about what's happened. But you cannot find freedom in the past, because it's already happened.

Now where can you find freedom? That must be what's next. That's the *good* news. The *bad* news is that what is next is unknown. Your freedom—your complete, total, final, and absolute freedom—lies in the vast realm of the unknown. To enter the unknown you must leave everything you've accumulated, *including* the wonderful peacefulness of the present, which in the end is just one more experience, just one more construction of the mind.

You won't find meaning in what's next. You cannot find meaning in the unknown. When you find meaning you know you're in mind. This is what's very delicate and dangerous about stepping into the energy of life instead of the description of the energy of life—without meaning we have no location. Without meaning we don't know who we are, or *where* we are. While we step into something that is totally alive, that which is totally alive does not need to reference *me*. Everything about my mind references me—it gives me meaning. When I step past that into something that is not referenced by me, I'm in a vast energetic realm and I can't find any meaning in it until I *construct* the meaning. I think, "I must be enlightened." Now I have meaning. Or, "I must be insane." Now I have meaning. The question of the human condition is: Do I need meaning to function? When you enter into the realm of meaning, you enter into the realm of dogma or belief—whether it's religion or philosophy or politics. This divides the universe into two things: everything I believe and everything I don't believe. Me and you.

So how do we get to something that is not divided? We have to leave meaning, and we have to leave location. No problem?

I'd like to tell you there is a road, but there is no road.

Consider this—the road of spirituality is all about cause and effect. If I meditate I become peaceful. If I do the right yoga I'll have a certain type of energy. What we're talking about is not in the realm of cause and effect. So not only is it without meaning, it's without causation. Consider how the manifest world actually takes place—it takes place in a moment without something before or without something after. You have to at least have something before to have something after—to have a system, a way, a process. But if it is in fact an energetic universe in which energy simply occurs without causation, not only is there nothing to do, there's nothing you *could* do. The doing is doing *you*. The energy is manifesting *you*.

We learn from the time we're babies that there is a before and an after, cause and effect. In the world of time and concept there are beautiful ideas, such as evolution and Newtonian physics, that we've all learned and agreed upon. Two hundred years ago we had a different set of ideas, and two hundred years from now there will be a *different* set of ideas that we agree upon. This is called reality—it's a set of concepts that we agree upon.

Scientists who look at the quantum level, the very tiny level of life, will tell you there's absolutely no causality. There is nothing that comes before, there's just energetic occurrence. Once a particle has occurred that had nothing before it, we can say, "It occurred." We can agree that it occurred. We can even say that a lot of particles that were occurring became a monkey, which became a man. This is the mind—it sees in the past. Now I say that I met a woman like you once and she was really mean to me. This is also the past nature of thought. I've got to be very careful what I say to you now because last time, in that past relationship with the woman like you, it really hurt. Then I wonder how I can get free of feeling hurt by a woman like you. And then I go to a class on being in the present. This is after I go through many years of psychological work, of course. And I find out it's the imprinting from my mother that is causing me trouble with women, but now I want to be in the present so I start learning how to do that. I start to watch my breath coming in and going out, but I'm still looking in the past.

This is *all* the mind looking back. Freedom doesn't lie "back there." You can apply anything you want from the past—it won't change what's next. The particles that collected into this group, into this world, are occurring without *any* causation at all. We can continue to look back and say it's the present, but the present is what's next.

THE SUBTLE DEEP FEELING THAT PULLS US THROUGH LIFE

Why do you want to stop the mind? This seems like some spiritual idea you learned someplace. You notice that you spend the first twenty years trying to start the mind in school, and then the next twenty years trying to stop the mind in your spirituality. Why do you want to stop the mind? How will you find your way home tonight?

Why don't you just disregard the mind's endless babbling? Why do you care what this mind is talking about?

You're not going to stop your mind. Just know that your mind is going to be there generating thoughts. The universe is generating thought. The universe is generating a left arm, head, thought, light, floor, this whole show, and you have absolutely no idea what any of that is. You just have your concepts. So why don't you find out what that stuff is, and then see if you want to get rid of it? If I don't like my left arm, how do I get rid of it? And how do you find out what all that is?

You're not going to get better. You're not, and definitely not in this room. What we're dealing with is not better or worse—we're dealing with what is. We realize that the world that we're dealing with is a world of mind generated in the past. Yet we know with absolute certainty that life takes place in what's next, and we can't access that using the conceptual mind. So now we say we want to get better. Does that mean we want to get better in the past, in the conceptual mind? How do I get better in the past?

The idea of improvement is another illusion of the psycho-spiritual world. There is no self-improvement. You can't get better. There's no better. But fortunately there's no worse either.

To explore these questions, to really step into them, is to go into energy. Not location, not meaning, not time. You can't possibly get anything from that. Do you see how uninteresting it is? *You* don't get anything out of that. Yet that's where life is happening. It's not happening in your past—life is not there. You have the world you create through your concepts— which is non-existent, dead, *finished*—that you occupy your entire life with. But even though you are squandering your life on illusion, at least you have *you*. Then you have this vast life that's highly energetic, vital, moving, dynamic, that doesn't have anything to do with you, doesn't care about you, doesn't refer to you. What would you like to explore?

I know what I would like to explore—I'd like to explore

me. Let me tell you about *my* life. This is where I want to go and this is where you want to go, and we could create a spiritual movement. Let's call it evolutionary conscious-ness—that sounds like something unique. But no way do I want to go into anything that doesn't involve me and what I know, what I've learned, and all my problems, my futures, and my pasts.

No matter what you take on in spirituality, what's next will always be the energetic movement actually taking place. In referencing the past you're referencing your own con-struction. What you're looking for in the past isn't there. You don't have to make the past go away—you *can't* make the past go away. But if you're looking in the past for what's next you won't find it. Can you go into your resistance, your past, without giving it the names you give it? Without construct-ing anything around it? We're so trained to look at aspects of ourselves as bad and imagine that there's something we're not getting that's good, when everything that occurs is just as it is. We have no meaningful way of judging it, because that judgment is the past. You can't possibly know what the meaning of your resistance is, or that it should go away. The only way you can know that is by referencing the past and applying it to that resistance.

It is very very confusing. And that confusion is a very beautiful state of mind, because in that confusion you can-not judge yourself as a person. There's no place to stand to say, "I'm doing okay" or "I'm not doing okay." If you cannot judge yourself, then you're in an energetic state. That state of deep feeling can be contracted or restricted as a description, or beautiful and wide open as a description, but let's be clear that those descriptions are the judgment. What is really going on is moving energy. The resistance, the naming, the judgment is the creation of the reality of the manifestation of the world out of that energy.

That's the world we see—the world of the past, the world of judgment. Without that judgment, resistance, and concept there would be *nothing*. There would be *no* manifestation; manifestation *is* the resistance to that energetic movement. Without time, without location, without meaning, there is nothing, and clearly there is something. Nobody lives in nothing. We all live in the manifest world. We live in the resistance, that border where resistance and energy meet as one.

You don't have to do anything, and you can do anything you want. You can meditate, you can stand on your head, you can dance. The energy is what's doing. The mind imagines itself as the doer, and then worries about whether it's doing the right thing. The energy is the manifestor. You can relax—or not. When it makes a difference, when it's important—I've got to do it right—that's the sense of meaning. But the energetic movement does not care about your conceptual doing. We have no meaning any more.

If something is without cause, then all things are without cause, and yet there's a manifest world. The brain researchers indicate that the sense of awareness, the doership, comes from a brain structure that distorts the sense of time. The movement to take an action comes first, the awareness of it is second, and in that awareness comes the time warp or twist that makes us think that the awareness came first. Imagine if your brain actually structured your awareness so that you saw clearly that you were aware of everything that you were doing only *after* it happened. This is what's actually going on. We're moving about and becoming aware of those movements only after they've already happened. Awareness structures itself as *before*.

I find my own ideas to be quite stale. If I had to live in just a world of my ideas and your ideas, this would be a pretty dead world. Where I find life is in the energetic movement and not in the old ideas. The question is not about making those past-their-sell-by-date ideas better or making them go away. I have a very driving question in me, which is, "Can a human being live an energetic life, in which the attention is to the energy and not the stale ideas?" I don't really know if that's possible. This is the experiment. Everyone will, in their minds, either like it or not like it. That's how habitual we are. But I wonder if we can go into this energy and live in an energetic way. Can we reference that subtle deep feeling that pulls us into and through life, and give expression to it in our everyday lives? We have no idea what that means. *You* don't have any idea and, in full disclosure, *I* don't have any idea either. So we're all in that experiment. We can't know how to do it from the past. We have to invent a whole new way of living with each other.

RELATIONSHIP IS ON FIRE

The word energy means many many things. You can throw out the word, and you can throw out the many many things. Still there is something, not nothing. When you throw out every single thing—every idea, every feeling, every emotion, every thought—there is still something, and that something has direction. It has movement, and that movement is the movement of life. I don't have any other way to talk about it, and I recognize that every way that I *do* talk about it has to be discarded.

Silence is a wonderful, beautiful, essential quality, and in that silence emerges action. That action, that movement, is the energetic quality. On a micro-level silence is emptiness, and action is the emergence of form. On the macro-level silence is the beautiful space we create in our meditation, our retreats and our dialogues. In the return to our lives—our husbands and wives and children, bills, jobs, society—the movement of manifestation is the question that emerges from silence.

But by the nature of the movement back to life, you must leave stillness in its entirety, to the point where you have forgotten about it, until the movement, the action, the manifest world is so rich that it covers over *all* the silence. It becomes so heavy that it begins to break down itself in the pain of the heaviness of form, decaying under that weight down to nothingness and stillness again.

You see this in every moment, in the movement of life on the macro-level. You cannot live a vital life in silence. You have to leave the silence to live a life. You have to abandon it, otherwise you're stuck in it.

It is a very dangerous question, to ask whether or not you are fully living a life. To find out you have to leave the silence completely. You have to abandon the reference to the silence. No talking about the silence, no experiencing the silence, no receiving the silence, no meditating on the silence.

Go into the separation if you want to find out the truth about silence. This is the challenge of the spiritual world—we have to move beyond spirituality to find out anything that's true. We have to leave the form that we've created.

When you subtract everything out, whatever is left is generating the whole show. You don't have to do anything. You're trying to *understand* it, and it's not in the realm of understanding. You can't feel it and you can't understand it. It's not the feminine and it's not the masculine. It's not in time, it's not something you can get to. So what is there for you to do? You're doing it. There's no improvement. It's already happened.

Now, *where* is it happening? *What* is happening? If there's no location, no meaning, no time, then what is that? So live from that. You already are. Let's see what we can manifest and what we *do* manifest.

You already have the perception. The pretense that you don't gives you something to do with your time. It's the great spiritual journey. But the spiritual journey is over, and now we're in a post-spiritual world.

I'm following the energy, and if it makes me contradict every sentence I say, then okay, I'll contradict every sentence. It's not a philosophy. The relationship from human being to human being is on *fire*. Each flame is different.

Human relationship is like a lava flow. It's energy, it's consciousness, it's manifesting without causation, and in the contradiction it's like chaos. You look at chaos and you find a pattern. If you look at contradiction you find pattern. And if you look at pattern you find chaos. This is paradox. The manifestation of life is resistance and energy meeting in paradox. Concept likes to fix paradox. It does not like the world where there's no resolution.

WHAT SHALL WE CREATE?

Let's relax. Let's forget that we're spiritual and remember that we're human beings. Do you recall that human beings often make mistakes? They often fail. They're not perfect. Spirituality suggests perfection. The expectation of perfection generates stress, very similar to the stress we got involved with spirituality to relieve. We're stressed at work, so we come to a spiritual place to relax, and now there's stress because we aren't spiritual enough.

I have resigned as a spiritual person, having earlier resigned as a spiritual teacher. In this post-spiritual reality I am simply a human being. So we don't have to pretend. We can be completely honest in a very simple way.

What I would like to know is, what is it that is deep inside of you? What would you like to express? What would you like to feel? What would you like to show? Not because it's important or special or spiritual, but because it's authentic, because it's actual, because it's passionate. That's the life that's important. We could talk about whether there's a self or no self, free will versus no free will, and endless important topics. Or we can get to what's important in our actual life.

What's *really* going on? Take away the spiritual idea—pretend you never went to a spiritual talk in your life. Spirituality is like the myth of the emperor's new clothes. The emperor says he has new clothes, and we have to pretend that there's some special thing—enlightenment, oneness, and so on. Those are the new clothes. We've all agreed to see that. The emperor wears the special clothes, not us. But if the new clothes of spirituality are in fact in our imagination, then the emperor is in fact standing there in his underwear. We're all standing there waiting to see who will be the first one to state the truth. So let's each one of us be the first one to state the truth, and as the child shows us in that story, the truth is what you see. Without any envy, without looking around for agreement, without considering what will happen if you speak the truth. *You* are responsible. *You* are. Whether you're a self or not a self, whether it's free will or not free will. You're it, and so am I.

It's not just that you don't *have* to change yourself, it's that you *cannot* change yourself. That realization is your freedom. If you can simply give up improvement, then all the stress and all the pain and pressure becomes something else. It's not that these things go away, that we can have a stress-free or pain-free life, but these things come as part of the life-stream, not as something to fix.

So what will you do with your life if you're not busy fixing yourself? This opens up a big question about the creative life, a very different question than how do you get enlightened.

An immense amount of life energy is available to live a creative life. When I don't spend it on fixing something that is an illusion, it is just as it is. It's radically simple. Let's declare the end of all special people, and let's all be common people who are just as we are. Now let's set about creating what we want to create. When we come up against a barrier or resistance, that is just what it is. When it releases and opens and energy flows then *that* is just what it is. You'll start to see an interesting thing—that resistance and energy are the same thing. This is the full range of life, and we've been trying to force everything into one tiny range of life—peacefulness, flow. But life isn't like that; life is like it is.

The thing we've been chasing we already have. The question we've been asking isn't the question we *need* to ask. The real question is, if life is just as it is, what shall we create? It's not doing nothing, it's what shall we do?

If I don't love right now there is *no* possibility that I will love right now, but that says *nothing* about what's next. What's next could be absolute love. But when I try to connect from this "not love" and push into what's next through some technique, some idea to get to that thing that I want, it doesn't work. It would be more accurate to say, "I don't love." There's *no* way, *no* way to what's next. What is next does not come from what's been. And this is very beautiful actually. This is why the reference to the past is so utterly useless, because in the next moment everything may change—I may love completely.

It doesn't come from anywhere—it's *not causal.* Nothing before it, nothing after it.

You can finish your process of transformation right here and now. It's very simple: never refer to the process of transformation again. The idea of transformation is finished.

The whole spiritual game is a scam. It's an operation that attempts to extract value in return for nothing. Pretend that we're in a real estate seminar and I'm going to sell you building lots in Hamburg, but I don't own them. That's a scam. Now the spiritual con is that I'm going to sell you building lots in Hamburg and not only do *I* not own them, but *you* own them *already*. I am selling you something you already own. This is the awareness game. How do I convince you that you're missing something so you can pay me to give it to you? You already *have* it. You're already aware, you don't have to buy it from anyone.

If you want transformation, live a creative life. Risk that life every moment through creativity and love and connection and speaking the truth. As aware human beings responsible for this life, what are we going to create together?

I'm asking you to actually step into that "what is," and see if it has anything to do with your concept of it. When I step into that energy, it's nothing like what I thought it was. It doesn't care at all about my ideas. It doesn't care at all about free will or no free will, or any philosophies.

The life force could produce anything, including transformation, change, something completely and radically new and different. If it is a field of all possibilities, then everything's possible.

Go into it directly. If you think you have no free will, than *live* that "no free will" and tell me about the energy. Not from the conceptual self, but from the energy itself. Speak from what is. We imagine that what is, is silence—we've been *told* that what is, is silence. When we get to this idea of what is, we become paralyzed. I'm saying that what is, is energy. Energy can speak, it can live and work and have families. It *is* that. It *is* the ordinary manifest world that we're living in.

That silence that you *can't* speak, that can't function in an ordinary life—*this* is an idea. If you want to see the quality of what you see, go to what is manifest.

A WILD PLACE

Are we willing to take the labels off ourselves? Labels protect us from feeling fear and confusion. But to get to a place without reaction to fear you're going to have to get really fearful. You have to go *into* your fear.

Why does life generate fear? Why do we respond to fear by trying to cut ourselves off from it? More fundamentally, what is fear? What is it that we run from?

Is it possible that fear is accurate, and that we can't handle whatever makes us fearful? Is it possible that fear is intelligence? I know we're supposed to face fear, that it's a choice between fear and love, but if you take the label "fear" off, what is it? Stop naming it and just experience it.

We divide up the energy of life using concepts, and call it fear and longing. In that world of ideas, we say that fear is stopping us from having what we're longing for. But those thoughts or concepts aren't actual. The energy you're feeling is actual, so can you stay with that feeling? You don't have to call it anything. It's not an experience. It's not special. It's not fear and it's not longing.

We cannot handle the energy. The energy is handling us. So let it. You can try to manage it by naming it, resisting it, working with it, going through all kinds of processes, but in the end you can't handle it. *None* of us can handle it. That's why we're here, the losers. This is the losers club, because we can't handle it and we know it. We're lost in the wild woods of life.

Energy is not efficient, it doesn't necessarily make your life better, it doesn't really care about your life or your efficiency. The conceptual structure that we create in our minds cares about those things, because I care about me, how am *I* doing, am I efficient, do I make enough money? I care about me because I've constructed that. But the energy of life, totality, consciousness, does not care about the individual construct because the individual construct is simply a construct. So who cares about your efficiency?

You don't know whether you will become the most efficient worker ever because the energy is flowing. We will not let the fact that we're lost be what we live from. We think, "I'm not lost, I know what I should be, I should be an efficient worker." But if you are truly lost, then you don't know how you should be. You can ask me and I'll tell you, you can ask your friends and they'll tell you, society will tell you, the schools will tell you, the police department will tell you. Lots of things will tell you how to be but these are also constructs, and you know that.

There are no shortcuts. You're lost in the woods and you

want a shortcut—to where? Where are you going? It takes all our energy to keep ourselves disconnected from the energy, disconnected from feeling. That's why we have relationship issues, because we're putting all our energy into separation.

Anyone who has toyed with madness knows that the constructs are constructs, that's what they've seen. They've seen beyond the veil of those constructs. It's a wild place. Whether we admit it to ourselves or not, it's a wild place. Whether we think, "I'm ready to go with the energy" or not, we're going with the energy. That's what's actually happening. We are actually lost in the woods. We can say, "I think where I'm going is over that mountain," and we can head for where we think that mountain is, but we're going in a direction that we don't know, whether we *think* we know or not.

If you have no reference at all, there is also *not* the reference of being lost. Being lost has to have a reference, and the reference we use is the ideal self. We refer to who I *should* be—what my mother told me, what society told me, what I tell myself I should be, how I can improve myself to become an ideal person. I have the enlightened being I'm supposed to be on top of everything else. I'm supposed to be successful, I'm supposed to have good relationships, contribute to society, be recognized, keep the bills paid, *and* be enlightened. This ideal self is the reference point, and then I think, "I'm lost" because I'm not *that*. But take that away. Take all the references away—are you lost? Can we be so lost that we're still? There's nothing to refer to that we should be.

We're supposed to see that the self doesn't exist. So now I'm stuck with *one more* thing to improve because I don't really get it. I think I'm me, I've got this body, the bills come in every month, my kids yell, so I'm pretty convinced that I am. Now I hear or read that this isn't true, and these clever speakers come through town and suggest to me that *they've* seen that the self doesn't exist, it isn't real. So now I think I'll sit and listen to these talks and I'll get that thing, that final thing. This is going to be the thing that trumps all the other things that I didn't get.

Now I'm chasing the "this is it" experience. But *that* isn't it, *this* is it, and *this* it is simply me chasing *that* ideal. It's just the merry-go-round of the mind. There's no improvement. This is what the mind does; it searches within its own realm for the experience that is beyond itself. The mind is constantly cranking through its own constructs looking for the escape from its own constructs. You'll never change it. You'll never improve it.

The only way you can change it is to destroy it. Go bang your head against the wall and you'll stop thinking, if you do it hard enough. But so long as there's thought, then thought will have these notions built into itself. All we're doing with spirituality, philosophy, and psychological is toying with constructs of mind. That's all. It doesn't make any difference whether you call it spirituality, the workplace, philosophy, shopping, or relationship—it's just a big field of concepts. There's no out, just like there's no in.

Spirituality is a paradox, but isn't it a boring paradox? It was exciting twenty years ago, and ten years ago it still had a little energy, and five years ago there wasn't much left but I was still willing to say it was a paradox. But, come on, life is going by. How many years are we going to spend playing in the spiritual world? Well, as many years as you would like. Some people like movies, some people like novels, some people like spirituality. But I'm bored with it. So what's post-spiritual? What's next after now?

The price of investigating the post-spiritual reality is your spirituality. You have to give it up. If you don't want to give it up, that's fine, and you can investigate spirituality. There are lots of people doing that.

What's the inquiry, what's the exploration when the personal spiritual journey is irrelevant? Or should we be dealing with improvement? We're used to the subject of getting better. So do we still want to get better? Are we making enough money? Should we have a better job? Are our parents proud of us?

What about happiness? Do you want happiness? The great goal of all this self-improvement is that *I* get to be happy. Let's be clear on this—to investigate, to explore the totality of life, we have to go *everywhere*. It can't be about sorting the experiences for what I like and what I don't like. This is the subtle reason for all the self-improvement. I would like my life to be the way I would like it to be. That's great, but it only allows me to explore that *part* of life, not the rest of life. We say I want to be happy, and what we're really saying is that I would like life to show up in a particular way. What you have to let go of, not as an action, not as, "I should let go of this," but what has to simply be exhausted is the notion that you're going to collect around you the things in life that make you happy.

What we're inquiring into in post-spirituality is very radical, because now I am no longer improving myself, including the fact that I'm stuck with a sense of self, the fact that I'm fearful, the fact that I feel lost and I refer to where I should be. I give up improving all those structures. I'm back to the beginning and I don't have spirituality anymore. The mind is still cranking away, the body is still there, all the constructs are there. I don't have the luxury of being crazy; I don't have the luxury of being spiritual. I don't have any authority I can look to inside or outside myself to help me. I'm beyond help. I've given up on improving *anything about me.*

Let us say that I love science-fiction novels. I get into one of those thick 800-page ones in which worlds are created, and spaceships arrive, and civilizations evolve, and I get to the last page and that world is over. I look up from the book, look around at my life, and I think, "This life of mine isn't very interesting, I'm just an average guy on planet earth." Do I pick up the next novel, because that's where the color and texture is? Or do I look around at what I am? We can imagine a new version of spirituality if you want. It'll be full of color. But at some point the science-fiction novel process itself becomes uninteresting. It's just one more universe being created, and I don't want to enter imaginary worlds anymore. That's what I'm calling the post-spiritual world. I don't know anything about it, actually. I'm just going around the world looking for people who might know something about it or who might be interested in investigating it with me.

I know a *lot* of things about spirituality. I could probably give a crackling talk on spirituality—mind arises, reality gets created, space, consciousness, time, movement of thought as time, on and on and on. It would make a good talk. But that world doesn't have any energy, so I have to go where the energy goes. If the energy goes left, I go left, if it goes right, I go right. There's no energy in spirituality. The energy is in something else.

Shall we find that out?

The personal journey, the journey of me getting better, me getting enlightened, that journey's over, and I didn't get better and I didn't get enlightened. The journey's over, it never began, it never happened at all.

If it's not about me because *my* journey really wasn't relevant anyway, it never actually existed, it was just an idea that I cooked up that I was going to get better, enlightened, superior, improved. If that disappears simply because it runs out of energy, what am I left with? I'm left with something that is not me.

How do I investigate that? I can't do it alone, because there's no me to investigate it. The spiritual journey—I can do that myself. I can go sit in a cave, I can meditate, I can push through it, I can see my mind, I can get into the experiences, God will come to *me*. It's really an individual quest, even though we're talking about getting beyond the individual. It is the individual who's on the spiritual journey. It's a heroic journey and I'm the hero in *my* story. *You're* the hero in *your* story.

Now we are not heroes, we're losers, the story's over, there's no place the story goes. What's left? From the perspective of the hero in *my* story, what's left is nothing. If it doesn't involve me there's nothing to it. There's no story past that. The post-spiritual world is in fact gray, because I don't get to be the star of it. That's it, it's over. Or is it?

DO YOU WANT TO BE HAPPY?

Welcome to the post-spiritual reality. We don't know anything about it.

We have to step out into what's moving, instead of *watching* life. The witness position is a safe place, nothing can touch me there. That's great, but that's also the tragedy of witnessing my life—nothing can touch me there. I'm going to step *into* life where *everything* touches me. You don't have to do that. You can stay back from life. You're safe. I can't get to you there, *nobody* can get to you there.

There's no "give it a try" here. That's like standing on the cliff and looking over and saying, "I think I'll try jumping off." There's no "try"—you jump off. There's no rehearsal, there's just the jumping off. I'm on the way down and I don't know whether I'll hit those rocks down there or the wind will come and blow me to a new place—but if you'd like, come on.

I have no idea how you do it, but it has something to do with the place of safety beginning to feel dead. Does it feel alive to you? For the watcher, the movement of life is happening *out there*. The place of the watcher is untouched.

This is the beauty of meditation—you don't have to be touched by anything. You can practice, you can go away for weeks and be untouched by the pain in your knees and everything going on in your life. This is great power, we think. It gives us a sense of control, doesn't it? See if you want to join life. You'll be touched by everything, and some of it feels good and some of it feels bad. There are no guarantees.

Bad things may happen, they may not. They *did* happen in the past and this is why we hide out in the witness place. This is intelligent. If every time I see you, you punch me in the face, then when I see you coming I'm going to hide behind a tree. That's intelligent. How do I convince myself to step out and see if you're going to punch me or not? I'm back there hiding, hiding, hiding, but at some point hiding is worse than getting punched. Everybody feels that they're going to get punched if they step into life. This is why we hide. I'm not saying that's not true. We may all come out of here today and think, "I'm going to step into life" and then, wham, we get knocked down.

That is why the question is, "Do you want to be happy?" If you want to be happy, stay behind that tree and hide and tell yourself you're happy. Here is an aphorism—"There's something fundamentally conflicted with wanting to be happy." What will you do with such a statement?

If you want to be happy, then you want to be happy. This is the fact of it, and certain directions come from that. Movements in history and philosophy have suggested that wanting happiness is wrong, and these movements don't usually work out too well. If you want to be happy, then you *do* want to be happy, and you'll take the actions that you think will produce happiness. But *my* question is, "Is that what I want in my life?" The pursuit of happiness, the collection of experiences, the pushing away of what I fear—is that what I'm really looking for? I'm interested in the *total* exploration of what life is.

I'm not suggesting that there's a choice about anything I'm talking about.

From what I can see, the energy of life doesn't care about your particular subjective experience of happiness. It just doesn't care. So the limitation of your world is the limitation of the bubble that you define as your happiness. If you're happy there, fine. The problem with that is that as soon as we see that it's a bubble, it's not happiness anymore, is it? When we're talking about happiness, we're really talking about the *idea* of happiness. The *fact* of happiness has no trace *at all*. There's no trace, we can't even talk about it, we can't refer to it, because it doesn't really exist. It's when "me" dissolves. The feeling of connection is the absence of me. I pull that back into my experience and I think, "I was happy and I'd like to be that way again." What am I chasing? I'm chasing something that *I* cannot have, all *I* can have is separation. You can stop chasing it, because you're not going to find it. But if you chase it, you chase it. That's why I talk about it in terms of exhaustion.

AWARENESS IS IRRELEVANT

It doesn't make any difference if you stay alert. This is the fraud of awareness. *Your* awareness is irrelevant. *Everything about you is irrelevant.* (And me too by the way, it's not just *you*.) *Any* construct of the self, my awareness, my wisdom, my greatness, my whatever, is irrelevant. Do you think that life cares about whether you're aware or not, whether you sat in some retreat and got aware?

If you want to look good in society then, sure, be aware. You won't do stupid things, you won't look like a fool, you'll probably work more efficiently, people will like you, and you'll have more social standing.

Let's start where Zen leaves off. In Zen you get enlightened, and you give up enlightenment to be a bodhisattva, and then what? This is the "what."

Step into the energy and see what happens. You don't

have to *do anything,* but let the energy move. The energy is what's animating you anyway. You're standing back from it with the idea that you're deciding to step into it or not.

DENIAL OF THE BODY

It's not that we can *decide* what to investigate. What we will *actually* investigate will be what actually shows up. What *has* shown up? Are we investigating how *I'm* going to get better? Are we investigating transactional energies, how the energy moves? Or are we investigating the end of time, nonexistence? If you're not in time, there's no transaction. There's nothing moving. There's no this and that, no subject-object, no nothing. This is nonexistence. Shall we go into that?

Faced with nonexistence, we whisper. Even in this room, when we're faced with nonexistence, we whisper. There's a murmur of existence. What we investigate is what occurs. We cannot investigate what isn't present. We *can* investigate what's present and we can't decide or control what that is. We can try to, but then we get into the conceptual framework. I can *convince* you that we're going to go into nonexistence now, and we'll all have an experience, but of course experience is not nonexistence.

Fear is a way of backing away from the massive energy of life, for the sake of survival. That is the function of the "me," and it's perfectly fine, because the organism *does* need to survive. But we've developed a whole universe around that "me." Just try to return to the body. Try to return to the actual functional me, which is in the body. Watch what happens, watch the resistance, the collapse of the psychological realm into the actual physicality from where it springs.

We're in denial of the body. We've created a disembodied realm in which we live, an imaginary world that has no existence. The body is the place we don't want to go. This is the functional me, the me that steps back from the truck coming down the street. Children have a very functional "me" in that respect. They're very body-centric, and their sense of what's in front of or behind them is very much in the body. But they're educated away from that simply because we tell them to be something they're not. I tell my boys all the time not to fight with each other. This is ridiculous, because their bodies are designed to fight with each other. They're boy bodies. They're not designed to *kill* each other, in fact they generally don't hurt each other, but they do fight. And I tell them to be kind and gentle, which they're not.

The body is a subset of the massive energy of life. If you look at it from quantum physics, there is no discrete thing called the body. If you look at it energetically, you can experience that this body is not really a container of anything. It's actually in dialogue with all other bodies. We don't look at it that way, of course, because we've learned about *my* body. This is the location of *me,* and this is how I will behave to be good. We've forgotten about the energetic reality.

CAN WE LET GO OF TRUTH?

Someone I know has organized his life around a certain perception of truth. Through the complete disintegration of his life, something emerged. That perception organized his life from that point forward, for thirty or forty years. I asked him whether that truth could be abandoned. Was it a limit to his exploration? I thought that question was pretty perceptive of me, but within twenty-four hours someone was bringing that very same question to me. Could I let go of *my* truth? Not my conditioning, not my habit, not my ego, not everything we know we're supposed to give up, but my *truth*. How do you give up your truth, how do you give up what you know, what your *perception* is?

This is not a truth that I decided to believe in, or

constructed by thinking about it or by going to teachers or reading books. The truth I'm talking about is the truth that *happened*. It's as though you wake up and see the sun rise, and you say the sun rose, and someone else says no it didn't. Can that truth go? Not the truth you construct. The truth you construct has to go, we know that.

To understand what I mean by unconstructed truth, let's presume a fairly astute yogi in this situation, one who checks in every moment to make sure that the truth is still current. He doesn't construct it, he's available to it being completely different, he even *expects* it to be completely different. In fact he doesn't even believe what that truth is suggesting, he sees it as impossible. He has let go of the truth.

Is there anything that has occurred to you in your life that has had certainty to it, that you didn't construct? Not certainty like "I really want to be an orthopedic surgeon"— not in that realm. This certainty is more like the perception that I'm *not*, that everything I know and construct *isn't*. I'm talking about a fundamental quality. Is there any fundamental perception that has occurred to you in your life? Not that you've built with your understanding, but that has occurred.

I'm using the word *perception* in the sense of the directionality of consciousness. It's meaningless to try and construct something that is not resonant with anything you can find. Certainty is inherently self-contained and self-satisfying. Certainty has already happened, it's not in time, not in process, it's already occurred. Do you have the certainty of your fifth birthday? Can you give it up?

Let's say that I have the certainty that this group of people has come together to facilitate world peace. I see in each of you the component that collectively will create world peace. This is like Jesus and the twelve apostles, a mystical collection.

The spiritual world is full of this kind of mythos. So let's say I had that certainty and each of you to some degree had some resonance with that vision, but also resistance to it, because we're embodied and we have personalities and we have families and jobs and so on. But despite my own doubt, my own confusion, my own personality and resistance to it, that certainty persisted, and I communicated that. And everyone said, "Is this guy crazy, is this an ideal, what's he talking about?" But something started to occur around that certainty and we worked with it. Some people are conscious that we're working with it to come to a fundamental perceptive field in which world peace could actually occur. Others think this is craziness and it's only about the struggle with the personal. There are different ranges of the perception.

But then one of you says to me, "Can you give up that perception?" The perception that *occurred*, not a perception that I built. I didn't say I'd like to have world peace, and then collected a bunch of people, and then I thought, hey, I'm a pretty cool guy. We're here and that perception occurred, you could *see* the peace in the world and somehow the human condition shifting, and this was the very *point* of being here. It wasn't some group of people who needed something to do on Sunday mornings. It wasn't about our personal problems, it wasn't about books or any of that. There was something more fundamental.

Or to use another metaphor, I'm the color yellow and somehow I'm able to fall back through the crystal prism into the white light, and I have the certainty that light in its essence is all spectrums. Then the color purple says to me, "Can you give that up?" How do I give that up? The perception is that it's yellow passing back through the crystal into the white light, which is clearly all the other colors. It's the unity of all manifest things.

My experience is that I can't lose the space, I can't lose the unitary perspective. That unitary perspective has qualities of timelessness and the absence of process in it. It is the actual movement of the light as it creates the play of colors. That's all there, it's occurred that way.

Can you give that up? If you *can* give up that metaphoric full light, then it's not real. From the perspective of the yellow, you can let go of the unitary perspective because the yellow is what remains.

If you're in the full light, you have all the attributes of it, which has a certainty to it. What actually seems to occur isn't the deconstruction of the ultimate but the deconstruction of the yellow, the limitation. *That's* the whole point. If in fact the full light perspective is actually what's occurring, it has yellow in it. It can let go of the yellow, the purple, anything, because it can create it easily enough when it needs it.

If we go back to the original metaphor that this is a group of people who've come together around the transformation of human consciousness, I have *no* capacity to get to that whole, transformational energy. But the gathering of these people is a different capacity, it's not just *my* capacity but *our* capacity. Does that change it? Do *we* have the capacity to experience something besides "me"? Do you have a greater capacity here than when you're walking around on the street? For example, when you're in love with another human being, is there a greater capacity in that than what's in you as an individual? A greater capacity to feel, to touch, to transform, to create?

When a perception is out of time and process—a perception of what we are already—then that begins to be communicated through form. Then the resistance to that will occur.

Some people will say that's completely crazy, some people will leave, some people will come, and reality churns around that perception. If the perception occurs, where does that come from? And does that not inherently create the thing it perceives?

This group doesn't have any purpose to it. It doesn't have any reason to be, other than it is self-creating each week. But it has the quantum possibility of being conscious of itself. Are we going to create world peace by going deeper and deeper and deeper into the human condition? Is this the commitment and the fact of our relationship together? (That's just an example; I'm not advocating for that.) Let's say you had that perception; that occurred to you, not as a construction. In this place, whatever you construct is going to get pulled apart. But let's say it *can't* get pulled apart, it's that clear.

Now I have to find my relationship to that perception, as does each person. If that perception is accurate, then this room forms around it. Why is that? Because the room either has to be in reaction to it or in agreement with it. We have to either join that perception and perceive it, or not.

This kind of perception isn't a psychic prediction. It is an occurrence outside of time that is magnetizing, bringing something forth, bringing it through time to that point. Do we have a relationship to that perception? How could we ignore it? That's such an intense energy that everyone has to have a relationship of some sort to it.

Is perception the active principle that catalyzes or is it in some way the alchemy? When consciousness decides to gather people together and moves through each and every one of them, that has a quality of amplification to it. If it's not happening in this room, then it's not happening on the whole planet, and this room is what I have access to.

149

The perception is the moving part, the form being transformed. In that respect it's totally fluid. The perception can move through the apparent paradox of the current situation, in which there's a group of people sitting around without an apparent purpose. Perception is still there. When people say the perception of that movement is clear to them, that they're in that perception, it's *still* there. And when resistance to that perception comes up—"That's not really right, that's cultic"—it's *still* there. The perception is not an intention; it is the movement through *all* those forms. It holds the reality.

It's a view of a deeper integration that isn't apparent but is already the expression of what is present. It's not in the future because it's not in time. The perception takes it out of time; it's the deepest integral perception of the circumstance. Is this an active force or not? Does it act on the apparent or does it just sit still as the recognition of the integrated space, and then the movement moves *toward* it through time?

When we talk about transformation from form to form, this perception is the next form before it's there. In quantum physics, it's probability—the movement. The actual occurrence is when the probability *becomes* the object or the thing, when the thingness occurs. Fluidity is the probability field, where anything can occur. But *something* actually occurs in that. Perception is how something occurs out of probability. It needs consciousness to occur.

If we just sat together over and over again, something would occur. Something would unfold from that. Do we just sit together and let things randomly happen? Is there anything else that gives direction or shape? Is there some perception in this group of people as to what we're doing here, or are we just going to let it fluidly unfold and whatever happens, happens? There's a capacity somewhere in this system for the perception to come to this group, to actually see the more integrated expression, and the seeing actually draws it into that shape. It has to be a perceptual group, a self-conscious group, that is completely fluid *and* completely conscious, so that it has both the stillness and the expression of stillness.

If you have a feeling or an intention, can you take that deeper? It's more about emptying out everything in *you* than it is about constructing something. We're on the brink of world peace, or world love, we're on the brink of all this. But what's actually happening is world annihilation. If you play out the mechanics of what's going on, world annihilation *is* taking place, in semi-slow motion, although it seems to be accelerating now. You wouldn't say that world peace is playing out, if you look at the geopolitics and the ecological situation and so on.

That feeling of being on the brink is a potent space. Go deeper into that feeling. There's so much energy there. That's the build-up of the potential. That's what I'm asking each of us and the group collectively to do here. Go into that on-the-brink space, because if we stay on this side of the brink then we are just in the mechanical process of showing up every week, and what unfolds in that will unfold. That's great, but there's something about going past the brink where this perceptual field takes place that is actually an accelerant. That's the quantum jump or movement.

You can feel how delicate the whole thing is, because it's very easy to make it into something. It's easy to create the illusion that something's occurring. Even hoping or wanting doesn't really apply at all. I can say I hope that happens or I want that to happen, or that's *my* purpose for being here—but none of that really actually applies. The perception *occurs*; this is the quality of it. You *can't* construct it, you can't make it happen, you can't *do* anything. When it occurs, it occurs in a way that's clear. It's unavoidable. It's an integrated force. All you can give up in that is the addiction to the personal, which is really what the demand of the integrated space is anyway, so the integration can go deeper. So, yes, I can give up the truth, not by giving up the perception, but by giving up the perceiver.

SILENCE

Words don't interfere with silence, words can *come* from silence. Find silence in yourself and see if any words occur. If they don't, you're just in silence. If they do, then they come from silence. Anything other than that is going to be leakage, noise, parrots squawking in the jungle.

Dialogue is what comes from stillness. The fluidity of that quiet space is sometimes words and sometimes silence and sometimes getting up and saying goodbye and going to whatever is next.

We have the great capacity as human beings to dissipate energy, and that dissipation is itself a kind of energy. I just went through several days that were really just a play of dissipation. I was in a gathering of people where dissipation was more the art form than anything else. That had its own richness in a way; it's a really remarkable thing. There's only so much dissipation you can take. At a certain point dissipation becomes focus. All qualities pass into their opposites or into something else. So you'll find that in a group that dissipates itself, the dissipation will actually dissipate the dissipation, and you come back to stillness. Then the stillness is refreshing, whereas before it was a pressure, which is why dissipation took place. It's as though the group as a whole thought, "I can't take that silence, so I'm just going to do something."

Even in a mundane life you can leave silence and go into dissipation, and if you really, really go into it, at a certain point the dissipation of a life becomes focus. You can't get away.

FEAR

We're often filled with fear about the details of our jobs, money, or relationships, but then we handle those issues and new fears pop up. We discover that we're not really afraid about those particular matters, but instead there's a constant undercurrent of fear in our lives. What is this undercurrent? Mind? Our parents' influence? The human condition? If we keep going with this investigation, what we're really stepping into is a deep, deep pool of energy, which is not about *my* circumstance. It's not about whether I have money, whether I'm doing my job well. That's what the energy attaches to in the mind, but when you think, "I'm on vacation and I'm *still* fearful, I'm sitting in a cave meditating now and I'm *still* fearful," what is that fear? You're touching on the energy of the human condition.

What should we do with that? Mostly what we do is think, "I don't want to be afraid, so I'm going to get more money, I'm going to do my job even better" or whatever it is we think will make us safe. We're chasing the resolution of fear by trying to fix it on the level of the symptom. Or we think, "I'll take a retreat or vacation and for a week or two I won't be fearful." Then I can go back to my life and be fearful, because I've relaxed a little bit. We try to fix it like that. But what if we don't fix it? What if we really touched fear as the human condition?

If we want to get rid of it, where are we going to put it? This is like our trash collection. We collect our trash in the trash can, we put it in the truck and the truck takes it, and what do we do with it? Where does it go? We bury it in a hole or we dump it in the ocean or we burn it. There's no place for it to go. It's still in the environment, isn't it? There's no place for fear to go; we can't push it away. We can *try*, but the question, "What is it?" is a question without an answer. There's no answer like, "Fear is (fill in the blank)." The question of fear is your own touching deeper and deeper and deeper into that energy. What you can see is what it's *not*. It's not about the money, it's not about the working, it's not about whether you're relaxed or not. This is the journey. There's no fix.

So you can't even call it fear, you can only call it energy.

Fear is a description, and part of that description is the idea that you're supposed to run away from what makes you afraid or do something to protect yourself. But in the energetic fact, you *are* that energy. This is power. But thought creates the opposite. If you approach fear through feeling, you will see that you already *are* it, you already *feel* it, you're already *there*. But if you approach through the image of your mind, then you have the sense of a choice—"I have to do something about what frightens me."

The name "fear" is the distance. The energy is already expressing itself. The energy of what we call fear is the action itself. You already know where that's going. That energy is intelligent—we've been *taught* that it's not.

If you touch into that energy as yourself, you touch into all energy, all selves. Then fear becomes something completely different. That energy is what you are, it's what we are. Form is the expression of energy. The mind will always pull you away from energy and feeling will always take you there—not the feeling of emotion, but the feeling underneath thought and emotion.

It's a question of where you locate yourself. If you locate yourself in the mind, trying to find the energy, then you locate yourself in fear. If you locate yourself in the energy, expressing the mind, then you're just looking at the manifest world as it is. The entire manifest world is in mind. Without mind, there's no manifestation. We're not trying to get rid of the mind. The mind is here. Anything that you can see or know *is* the mind. What I'm calling energy is what you *cannot* know, what is beyond the known. Its expression is what we know. Where we locate ourselves is in the mind, but where we're actually located is in the energy, whose expression is the mind.

FEELING

It's very simple—life is what it is. I'm not suggesting you should be at peace with what is. I'm saying it doesn't make any difference *how* you are in relation to what is. It still is what it is. If you're not peaceful with life, it still is what it is. I'm not patient with what is. I know it's not going to *change* what is and I also know that that is the energy expressing itself through me, just as each person in this room is a different expression of the energy. I'm not going to improve my impatience any more than I'm going to improve what is.

It's not about being peaceful, although if you *are* peaceful, wonderful. Every once in a while I'm peaceful, and I think it's great—I usually mark it on my calendar. "Oh yeah, this was a peaceful moment." We've tried to take pictures of it, but it doesn't come out.

Once we start working on a feeling, it's not the feeling anymore. This is very tricky territory. If we try to work on a feeling, suddenly we have an object, a thing. The feeling stops being something fluid and becomes fixed, and not only that, but we have the dynamic of you and me, and the dynamic of the room. This is a spiritual trick. Someone says, "I want to work on feelings," and a guy like me says, "What's the feeling?" and suddenly the feeling is *not* the feeling you were talking about. Now it's the feeling of being focused on in a group of people where some guy has the power and you don't. If I'm good at what I do, I can talk to you as if we're working on the feeling. Even if we clear out the room and it's just you and me, there's still that dynamic. Even if it's just you alone, there will still be an interpretation—what the feeling is, what it should be, and what it shouldn't be. For example, if you call the feeling irritation, in the world of spirituality that's a negative. But if you use the word energy, it's positive, as in, "I was feeling a lot of energy around that question."

We're always characterizing our feeling using our concepts, and then we mix it into power relations—the power of the teacher, the power of one in a group, even the power of our own mind characterizing those feelings. Energetic feeling doesn't care about any of that. However we try to work with it, it shows up when it wants and it goes away when it wants. I would work on *feeling* feeling, not working on it. Nothing else is required—you don't have to name it, don't have to fix it. All feeling is energy.

You can't make suffering feel better—suffering feels like suffering. But you don't have to name it "suffering" and then try to fix it and alleviate it. There's *nothing* you can do. You can cover it over, you can distract yourself, you can name it all kinds of things, but that energy is still there. It's there until it's not there.

CHANGE

How do we know what to change about ourselves? There are so many things about myself I don't like (pretty much everything), so how do I know what to change? How do I know I'm not changing something that is actually creative? Yet we go to spiritual teachers to change ourselves. We take on spiritual practices to change ourselves. We think, "I'm too agitated, I want to be peaceful." Why do we do that? How do we know what to change? And how do we know what to change *to*?

My attempts to change don't work anyway. The whole idea of change is absurd when I'm the one that's changing things, like a politician running for election suggesting he will clean up the political process. But if I do absolutely nothing, I notice that things are changing all the time.

From the perspective of the self, change is a big problem. The *whole* attempt of thought is to fix life into a location—to create time, before and after, to give meaning. This is what thought does, and change threatens all of that. Seeing that threat, thought tries to control change.

I always want to change it so that *I'm* more comfortable. In my spiritual life that means to make it go really, really quiet, because in silence I'm comfortable and safe. But there's no silence. I can never get it to *be* silent. To put it another way, my silence is always under pressure. There's always something *intruding* on it. So even if I go away for a week and I do a silent retreat, I come back and there's my life waiting for me. None of our lives are silent.

What if I stopped trying to change things so that they're more comfortable? Not more comfortable for you, but more comfortable for me, and not more comfortable like a chair is comfortable, but more comfortable psychologically. What if I totally abandon this attempt? What if I accept that life is sometimes uncomfortable? Sometimes you walk into a room and it's uncomfortable, and you sit down in the chair as a speaker and it's uncomfortable, and you don't know what to say about *anything*, and that's *really* uncomfortable.

I come into the room and I find it all irritating—the way the light is, the noise, people coming in late—all these things are uncomfortable for me, and I have to make them comfortable, and now where am I? Am I still in this room or am I in some state of mind? In this room there was just discomfort, that's all, and if I don't try to change it, it changes. It changes the room and it changes me. That movement, that change, is what life is. All the efforts to control that, including our spirituality, are entirely useless.

Changing myself means that my whole frame of reference is different. If I'm still referring to who I *was*, then I really haven't changed. If I'm a person who is angry all the time and I think I'm going to be less angry, it's not really change. So if I really did change and I didn't reference the past, how would I know that I had changed? Change is the past look-ing for freedom from itself, but where it looks is always ref-erenced *to* itself, so it's impossible. If change is possible, you cannot know it. You cannot measure change. Maybe we've all changed tonight, but we can't know it. When we try to change through great effort, that is the past trying to refer-ence itself again. So do you still want to make a lot of effort? You *can*, that's okay. It's no problem. It's just not going to bring you what you think it's going to bring you. It'll fill up your life, it'll make you feel tired from trying, but change doesn't come from effort.

Change happens, and change doesn't care whether you're trying or not trying. So you can do absolutely nothing and you'll notice that life changes, and there's no reference to that. You can look back and you can say that "back" has changed, but you can't look forward and say it *will* change to a definite something. And that's very lovely, isn't it? Change can hap-pen and it can happen in any way. So why are we spending so much time trying to make change happen?

I invite everyone to do absolutely nothing about changing *anything*, and watch the change happen—because it's hap-pening all the time. My body's moving all the time. I'm tak-ing in information all the time. The flow of feeling is chang-ing, people are coming and people are going. I'm not *doing* anything to make any of that happen.

We can describe change, but we don't know what caused the change. Is it possible that we tell a story looking back, as a way of explaining to ourselves something that happened? But what happened, *happened*, and then we explain it. Some-thing did happen, but *how* it happened, *when* it happened, and *why* it happened is really a mystery.

It's possible we're in an energetic world that is very

difficult for us to be in, and so we construct a story, a location, a before and after—*this* because of *that*—in hopes of making sense of something that doesn't make sense. Maybe we can begin to live *comfortably* in a world that doesn't make sense. Maybe we're becoming comfortable with a world of feeling. We don't have to harden that world into the world of concept so quickly. We can begin to see the flow and movement of energy as it takes shape and as it breaks down and takes new shape. It doesn't have to harden into a me and a you necessarily. When function is necessary, function, but it doesn't become identity.

LIFE GOES EVERYWHERE

What we actually are is unrecognizable. The facsimile I've created of who I am is not who I am. To actually reside in the energy of what I am, and say I am that energy, is so devastating to the skin, to the facade of what I am, that it is death. It's the death of everything I know about myself and everything I've created around me. I'm afraid of insubstantiality—there's really nothing solid anywhere. It's complete annihilation, so I won't go there. Everything in me will resist that.

This is where the quality of grace comes in. If there's an animating quality in the universe, it's grace, which takes us into the annihilation, through it, past it. The skin isn't going to do it; the facsimile of who I am couldn't possibly do it. It doesn't have the means to do it, and wouldn't remove itself.

The skin, the facsimile, the artificial, the false, the picture of life is happy to cultivate itself all day long to get closer and closer and closer to enlightenment. You can't cultivate your way to enlightenment. We think awareness is magical and so we practice that, but awareness isn't going to help either; you're going to have to give it up.

If you live from the truth you perceive, the evidence of it will be in the relationships in your life that are in conflict. See if your truth lives in the relationships that are breaking down, the ones that are confronting you. Or see if it only works in special spaces, with agreeable people, spiritual people. What is alive lives no matter what. So if your truth lives only in special places, it's a special place truth, a relative truth. You have to go to hell, and if it's alive there in hell, then it's alive. If it takes you to heaven, and you don't get caught up in heaven, then it's alive. That's what life is; life goes everywhere. We just want to go to the good places, but life goes everywhere. It doesn't have a concern about the good and the bad, the heavens and hells.

JUST SURRENDER

If you'd rather eat junk food than meditate, then eat as much junk food as you can. Just eat and eat and eat and eat, if that's what the feeling is. So what if it's a pattern? It's a pattern you believe in apparently, so it's not a pattern, it's your life. But by making it a pattern then you can work on it and you can develop yourself around that. Then you can believe that you're not *really* that pattern. Well, welcome to yourself, you *are* a pattern, and there's no way out.

The pattern's not alive, it's a pattern. It eats junk food, that's what it does. That's pain. Now you're in contact with pain—you see yourself, you're a pattern, and that's it. That burns. There's absolutely no way out. You can try meditating, try this, that and the other thing, but pain is its own energy. Don't tell yourself it's okay. Pain is alive. That pain is the same as energy.

The way out is as simple as it is impossible to do. Here's an easy formula, just surrender. How do you do that? There is no way. Surrender comes out of grace. Simply surrender to the movement of energy and let it rip, let it change the face of your universe, let it be the expression of who and what you are, and accept that you are that energy. Well that's all great, that's a nice line and you could do a good book on that. But how do you do that? The fact is you don't, you can't. You can *talk* about it, you can go to people who will advise you on it, but the act of surrender is not an act of me, it's an act of grace, it's an act of the energy itself. So the energy itself picks even the mode of surrender, the moment when you pop.

There is no control in this. There is no *doing* in this.

It's not acceptance, because surrender also means that I push against certain things, that sometimes there's an active force of change. It can be passive and it can be active. Surrender means that I recognize that I am not running the show in any way. There's no hope that I'm going to run the show, it's just not a fact. And if life is running the show, this is a different life altogether.

ENLIGHTENMENT

Enlightenment suggests a special place that transcends the common experience. If you take certain actions you get there and then you're safe forever. If you feel like it you can come back and help the little people, but if not, that's cool too.

I see enlightenment on the contrary as plunging *into* the dualism of a common life, being affected by it, being consumed by it. It's actually a collision with dualism and it's transformational. Otherwise it's an inert quality, and who cares? Some guy is sitting around untouched, still, in Samadhi. Why do we care about that? He could be in a mental hospital as a catatonic or he could be on a cushion as a saint. Why would we be interested in that?

If you sent any of the enlightened people off to a restaurant with the three kids I was with yesterday, could they handle it? If it's not workable in an ordinary life, what good is enlightenment? You can get into amazing spaces and then come back into your life structure and the whole thing will be completely consumed within seconds. You can try to push the life structure into that space. You can ask the people around you, "Why aren't you more like I am when I'm in that space? Obviously you don't fit in this life, so go away. Only people who are in that space can stay around." Of course this makes it hard for many people to stay around. Eventually that question reverses itself: "What am *I* doing?" It looks a lot like we are running.

It's impossible to integrate the big and small spaces, because they're both states of mind; they're both attempts to control life. What if you don't try to integrate them, but you simply surrender?

What's enlightenment if it's everything? This is when the word *enlightenment* has no meaning. It's everything we know, and everything we *don't* know.

What does enlightenment have to do with not knowing? I can't even say I know that I don't know, that becomes a stance also. I'd say *confusion* is a better word than *enlightenment*. The movement of confusion is really freedom. It's a surrender, because what else can you do? How do you organize confusion into something that's coherent, that you can explain or say?

Enlightenment is really the dissolving of the idea of enlightenment and any one to be enlightened.

The clarity we're looking for is that of infrastructure. The only clarity that's available occurs in the moment and arises out of the breakdown of the known. It arises out of the confusion of unknowing as the actuality of that moment. For that to be the case we have to be completely available to what is. We can't project the quality of what is, it might be clarity for all we know. But we can't *fix* that clarity, we can't make it into a philosophy, an ideology, a system that's going to go into the next moment and say *that* clarity is now applicable to *this* moment.

Desire is the movement of energy creating something. While it can seem like it's a bastardization of the movement, a disconnection from it, an attempt to stand outside that movement and control it, even *that* is an expression of that same intelligence.

The conflict we experience in desire is an apparition. It's not actual. You can't actually find conflict if you go *into* it, if you try to make contact, and *keep going.* You won't find conflict there, you'll find undifferentiated energy. The feeling of conflict is an illusion. We create irresolvable issues as a way of giving ourselves a location.

HOPE

Hope and hopelessness are aspects of the same thing. They're in relation to a picture of what we want to happen. Hope says, "I *think* it's going to happen," and hopelessness says, "It *isn't* going to happen." Both are in relationship to a picture, whereas the unknown doesn't have any pictures in it. It doesn't have hope *or* hopelessness in it. The quality of the unknown is that *all* things are potential. My particular idea or picture *could* happen, sometimes it *does* happen, and I get the thing I want, but it's part of a flow that has nothing to do specifically with my idea.

It's important to face the lack of hope rather than create the idea of hope or hopelessness. If you look directly, without hope, you see all possibilities. When you look with hope, then you just see one possibility. With hopelessness you see no possibility. Life is much more open than that. But the mind always wants hope.

We're structured so that we don't see that what we are is what we want. The whole thing is one thing, and we divide it up and think, "I'm not the way I want to be" so that we don't see that whole. Imagine a world in which how you are *is* what you want.

THE CREATIVE MOVEMENT

When there's a compression of energy and a release of it, a buildup of potential and then the expression of that potential, mostly we recognize the expression as creativity. But in fact the compression or the buildup of potential is also creativity. In this respect, I would say we are all always creative. Sometimes this doesn't appear very obvious because it's a quiet, empty, or compressed space. In that space we wonder how we can be creative, but it's the empty space before the expression.

Creativity is a space that you prepare to receive. The quiet space is how creativity builds up. You can't stimulate creativity, but you can stop beating yourself up about not being creative.

Form is the structure that we hold in our mind, in our relationships, in our society; and the energy is constantly creating *new* form. That's what it does, that's what the creative movement *is*. Our thought structure tries to keep it still, fixed, because we're afraid—afraid of losing the husband or wife or family or job or friends, and afraid of having them at the same time. So we either try to hold on to them or we think, "Ah that's why I'm not creative." It's the husband or wife or family. But that's not what stops the creativity— that's the *expression* of it up to this moment. When energy moves, the form of things may change. That change may be radical, and that's the risk of creativity that we often say we don't want.

You can see this very clearly in a spousal relationship. You can see this in social structures that depend on a certain belief or idea. If you just stay with the energy and take the risk of creativity, what's true in your life will travel through that energy, and what's not true in your life has already fallen away.

THE UNKNOWN

The unknown is not anything at all. There is no thingness in it. There is nothing there, no manifestation. The thinking mind cannot go there, yet the energy of life comes from the unknown and manifests *as* the thinking mind. It comes from nothing, so nothing causes it. We sit in the expression of that energy and act as if we can control the energy that comes from nothing.

You cannot *get* to the nothing. You can spend ten years in a cave where thought comes *very very* slowly, and you can press into that nothing, but as you go into the unmanifest, something pushes back. That is the energy of life. That pushing back is the creative energy. That's why there is a manifest world; that's why there is something and not nothing.

As we go through our day, we describe the shifting energy states to ourselves—relaxation, tension, confusion—but if we strip away the description and the positive-negative judgment, we see that these are just energy dynamics. They're not just in you; they may be in the whole space. Once you claim it as *my* tension or *my* confusion, then it attaches to "that's good" or "that's bad," and then you have all the correcting mechanisms. If it's bad I want to make it good and if it's good I want to hold onto it. Then you're into layers of story that are the expression of that energy. We can *see* them, we can *feel* them, it's very palpable, very real. But it's not the energy. The energy doesn't have any of those descriptions. The energy is like nothingness—it doesn't have any of those attributes at all. The closest we can get to it is very, very simple descriptions. We can call those simple descriptions *feeling*. Very, very simple feelings don't have any good or bad to them. Feeling uncomfortable or feeling tension or pressure or expansion or release—these are descriptions of the feeling but they're not qualified by the mind sorting them.

Can we live in the unknown? Is that intelligent? Can it organize life in a new way? Is it worth spending our life in that flow of feeling as a reference, as the organizing principle? We've spent so many years—centuries—organizing around the *conceptual* world: "I'm a man, I'm an American, I have these ideas, and I *protect* all that, and I *organize* like that." This is what we've been doing. Now more recently we've been thinking, "Well that's making me feel unhappy, I'm not so good with this, so I'm going to *change* it." So now I'm a *spiritual* American man. But it's still a concept. Then I find this thing called "silence," and now I'm a silent spiritual American man. But that silence is an idea, because you cannot get to real silence. There's no American man in that silence. There's no *manifest world* in that silence. So that's the end of spirituality. If I'm an American man and there's no spirituality as a way out, then I think, "Okay, then I guess I'm done. I'm not going to do *anything*." Then I start noticing that when I do absolutely nothing to fix what I am, life moves. It changes, it shifts. If I don't try to organize that shifting into a better American man, a newer American man, a special American man, then I'm just energy. Just like you— not better and not worse than you.

The categorizing of feelings and what's inside *is* what I imagine I am. What I like and what I don't like *is* what I imagine I am, and I cannot imagine a world without *me*. There's no way to imagine it, but you *can* live it. The mind is caught in its own referencing, it cannot imagine beyond itself. But that is not the limitation of our human potential. We *do* have the capacity to live in that energetic field. You don't have to imagine it, just live it. This is like the experiment of life—you don't have a description of what life is. Every single thing that we do has to change, and it *is* changing, so let's begin to live in that change.

We may think that we want to live in change, but then what about the bank account? There's tremendous resistance to that energetic life. It comes in the form of thought, as fear. But here's the trick: Look at it energetically, don't look at it from thought. Energetically, fear is energy—it's not resistance, it's expression. This is important. Fear is energy. When you look at it from thought, fear suggests all kinds of things in form and it will fill your mind endlessly with images, but when you strip it down to what it *is*, it's energy. It's energy with certain qualities, certain feelings, and it's dynamic and moving and changing. When you live in fear, you live in energy. You don't have to call it fear, you don't have to call it anything.

Change is energy, fear is energy—it's all contact with that energy. So when you're feeling, you know you're in contact with energy. I'm not saying it's pleasant, but it's alive. It's a very creative energy—it brings change to your system.

Even *fear* changes. Let's not even call it fear, let's call it energy and watch it change. Sometimes it's contracted and compressed, sometimes it's wide open, sometimes it drives us into action, sometimes it paralyzes us.

We can call it fear, we can call it energy, but it's a *gift*. It's a strange gift, but it's a gift. All these deep feelings we have are the gifts of life. It's a gift that's beyond liking or disliking—it's *that* vital, *that* essential to feel.

You can't control it. It's a subtle thing. There are so many magical occurrences in life, and rather than see them as completely magical we always try to organize them with *me* as the subject. Even on very subtle levels there's the attempt to organize the energy as something I control. This is the dangerous territory of spirituality. Because teachers have had certain experiences, they've deluded themselves into thinking they can control these things, and then they sell it to the students.

Many years ago a very well-known teacher was teaching out of a deep realization. Recently he revealed that after a few years of teaching that realization left, so he stopped teaching. Now how many teachers do you hear about that stop teaching? The energy moves and there's an opening and you think, "Oh, I must be enlightened." Maybe you are enlightened, but then you start organizing it and teaching it and you forget that you've lost it. We don't control the manifestation of the energy. The manifestation doesn't control what manifests it. This is why I say that the whole set-up of being a spiritual teacher is a very dangerous one. Sitting in that role, oftentimes I am not able to manifest the role of "teacher." I can *control* an audience, I can use power and force to dominate, I can use the position I have to make anyone look like a fool, but I cannot actually *be* a teacher. I don't control that, the energy does. So what I see is that energy can make me a teacher in *this* moment, but a student of *you* in the next moment. If I'm only willing to be your teacher, then I'm missing a lot of life.

Spirituality is actually a journey into the known. We go into what the teacher tells us to go into and listen to what he or she says about how to go there and what to experience. But what we're talking about is a journey into the unknown, and that's why there can be no teachers. How can you be a teacher about the unknown? You can't. All you can do is live.

My interest is in what's alive, and that's where I'm going. I can't tell you to go there, I'm *not* telling you to go there. I'm just trying to describe what I'm seeing. Perhaps we're inventing some new culture, and we're going to have to go there first, and if we become insane or incapacitated then people will say, "That's so sad." But if we invent new ways of living that are alive and intelligent, then maybe people will say, "That's pretty amazing that that happened." I can't reassure you, and I think that it is honest to be concerned about an unpleasant outcome of this exploration and the life that expresses from it.

RELATIONSHIP

If we form relationship from deep knowing, is rejection possible? In connection, you can say anything you want to me—*anything*—and there's no feeling of rejection. You can tell me that I'm the worst speaker in the world or that what I say is stupid, and we'll both see that as an energetic occurrence.

Or we could form a relationship in which I want something from you. I would really like you to like me, and not only tonight but tomorrow when I wake up and in the afternoon when I'm really grumpy and on and on. I want you to like me. But tomorrow when I'm ill-tempered, nobody in their right mind would like that. So tomorrow you *don't* like me, and then I feel rejected, and then I'm *really* irritable. Eventually we figure out that we really shouldn't be together. Where did this all start? I wanted something from you. When you form your relationship about wanting something from the other person then you've made a deal, and you can keep that deal for the first day or week or year, but eventually rejection will happen. So why not form your relationship out of the deep knowing and not out of wanting?

Life energy manifests a beautiful mechanism for showing us who we are in our conceptual world, that is, what I see is what I am. But we're really tricky—instead of saying, "That's what *I* am," I say, "That's what *you* are and *you're* the problem." So I trade *you* in for *her*, and now *she's* the problem, and then I trade *her* in for *her*. What's staying the same in all this? *I'm* the same. This is my mind generating the expression of my mind.

Don't tell yourself the story that you cannot form relationships out of your deep knowing. If you're going to tell yourself a story, tell yourself *this* story: I don't know. Because that's the fact. You don't know what's next. And that's your freedom. In that freedom you may create another prison, but it's just as possible that you'll live in that freedom.

Deep knowing, which I am using as another term for energy, doesn't really leave any trace. So you cannot know that you're living from deep knowing. All you can know is if you're not. The way you can know that you're not is the occurrence of thought. You'll notice when you're in conflict that there's a lot of thought. Then you can see that the action that comes from that conflict or that thought will be more conflict. It's like deciding between boredom and fear. You can think about that all you want, but the action doesn't come from the thinking.

Do you feel the energy of that space as your mind tries to understand and can't? That's the deep knowing, and the mind can't get there—it's a paradox. The intense, confusing space is the deep knowing. Follow that.

THE NEW OLD

What is *new?* Would you recognize it if you saw it? Sometimes scientists see evidence of something they cannot believe is possible, such as the existence of dark matter or antimatter, which is the opposite of matter. There's a lot of evidence for it, but when scientists first came across it they didn't see it as possible. Human beings can't actually see what is new. What we *do* see is the old and we *call* it the new.

If we can't recognize the new, then we are simply creating the *new* old—the same thing all over again. In the world of spirituality, it was *Be Here Now* in 1971, and more recently it's *The Power of Now,* and in thirty years it will again be something about *now.* We recycle this idea and we call it spirituality.

What mechanism do human beings have to recognize something new? Will *new* show up on our cat scan? Brain scientists can describe what happens when the brain makes new neurons, neurons that have not had any experience yet. These absolutely fresh brain cells receive their first impulse.

What is that first impulse? What does it look like? What does it taste like? What does it smell like?

It doesn't look like, taste like, smell like anything at all, but we place on it what we already know. This is the paradox: we don't have access to what is new. The only access we have to what is new is through what we know. We organize newness into what we know already, and then we either like it or don't like it. We judge it based it on what we know.

Whatever you know, you know that there's something that you *don't* know. It's the unknown. The known, the place where I am, is an old movie. I've seen it before, so many times. I know how it goes—I know who the heroes are, who the villains are, I know the ending. I watch it over and over and over again. This is what I call neurotic.

I spend a lot of time with my neurotic mind, which is everything I see. You are my neurotic mind as far as I'm concerned. That neurotic mind does not have the capacity to do anything but generate the new old. Most of us feel that the *old* old is good because we feel secure. Some of us who are really spiritual and adventurous say the *new* old is where we want to go. Our spirituality is about creating a new variation on the old that keeps us entertained. It's like going to the same romance movie but with a different actor and actress, so you know they're still going to fall in love and have some problems and in the end they're going to be happy.

Even in the so-called "now," the present is the past. The now is smoke and mirrors. The whole "now" industry is based on a fallacy. You can't *get* to the now, you can only get to the last now, the one before. That's where we live at our peak of spirituality. When we've spent twenty years practicing being present, and now we're *always* present—like beady little monks—we are present only to the *last* moment, the one before.

The new cannot be a description and it cannot create an experience. Experience is the past. *All* experiences—the most *beautiful* experiences, the wrenching, painful experiences, the experience of no self, the experience of silence—*all* those are the same. I've *had* the big mind experience, I've *had* the no-self experience, I've *had* the silence experience, I've *had* the transmission experience. These exalted experiences just piled up on top of all the other experiences—the experience of being embarrassed when I was in sixth grade, the experience of falling in love for the first time, the experience of my first cup of coffee—they're all in there. All the books I've read, all the ideas I agree with and don't agree with are all in there, along with the experience of no self, enlightenment, silence. I can pull out any one of those and say, "That's mine, that's me."

There is no such thing as a *new* experience; there might be something *new*, but it's not an experience. Experience has *me* with it.

I know that there's something I don't know, and that knowing of the unknown is the question of the new. Everything I could say about it is a combination of the old. It's not in the words. It's in something that is not in the mind structure at all. It's someplace else.

PASSION

Many of us have the feeling that something is missing from our lives. Why don't we live from that feeling then? If we do, then everything will change. That's what we call passion. But then the life of conditioning is gone. Nothing stops us from living from our passion, but we move from conditioning, not from the feeling. The feeling becomes something we talk about as dissatisfaction.

CONFUSION

Confusion is taking place in all lives at all times, and action doesn't come from the clarification of that confusion. When we stop a child from stepping in front of a car, we don't act from clarity or confusion, we act. The action comes from the immediacy, it doesn't come from any kind of construction at all. In fact it's only *after* the fact that we construct what happened.

The constructing mind doesn't tell us much about our life, it tells us about the reflection of our life in the mind and it tells us how we tend to occupy ourselves.

The actual life is taking place and *then* the description. It's happening so quickly that it looks like the description is the generator of life, and so we live in our description as if it's life, forgetting that life is actually happening. The mysterious life force is forgotten in our creation of worlds that we then spend our time winding and unwinding. We want the thing that feels good, and don't want the thing that feels bad. I try to convince whoever is in relationship to me to make me feel good by changing who they are, and by the way, I've created who they are as a description in my mind. This is a tug-of-war, except that it's me pulling against me.

WHAT ELSE?

You're not seeing what's there, you're seeing what your brain constructs is there. You think there's a table in front of you. There's a vast amount of space, there's energetic material that is interchanging all kinds of electromagnetic radiation; there's gravity pulling down and weaker gravity pulling up. You're seeing a very small range of color and light; you don't see anything about the heat that is radiating out of it. You put all that together into a thing called a table and you thump it and you think something is happening. Do you feel the vibration go through the floor all the way to the ground? That's what's happening.

If a snake were in the room it would be tasting the table, picking up little molecules.

Just like the snake, we're constructing a little tiny bit of the universe, but we cling to it very tightly, thinking, "I know where I am."

We could understand that as incomplete, but we understand that not only as something complete, but something we must defend to the death. When you see it as incomplete, then what is left is a question—What else?

LOVE

When we fall in love we always think we fall in love with a beautiful creature—this wonderful, smart, intelligent, person—and we think, *I'm* going to get *that*. That's why I'm in love, because I'm going to get that in my life. It's going to be absorbed into me. But what I actually get is love; I don't get that form at all. I get that person becoming old, ugly, poor, sick, not liking me—I get all the things that I don't want. And I get love. I have to love all those forms. It's not the form that I *thought* I loved, it's everything *but* that. If I saw that when I fell in love and I convinced this person that they should be with me because I *wanted* that, if I saw the aging body and the anger and all the garbage that I was going to be asked to love, would I be in love? Or would I move on to the next one?

Can we design a life of wholeness—a life that includes all the things we *don't* want? Am I prepared to live a life I don't want? Am I prepared to be a slave to the energy *knowing* it's going to take me to the places I don't want to go?

We're *desperately* trying to design a life that takes us where we want to go, so that I can have the experiences that *I* want that are pleasurable to me, I can get the young, the beautiful, the rich, the attentive, the admiring, all those things. That's what I want. Why would I go to the old, the decrepit, those who are critical of me, those who don't respect me—why would I go there? But that's where life's going to take me.

The beautiful part is invisible. What is beautiful in the things that I'm engaged in is only beautiful because I'm not. All I can have when I'm present as an individual, as a center, is ugliness. I can try to attract beauty to me, but the only way I can have beauty is to be absent. That's what beauty is—the absence of separation. This is the conundrum.

PARTICLE / WAVE

A group carries the cultic possibility of agreeing that something special is happening within it, and the subtle pressure for that specialness to continue. If I say something special is happening, and someone else says he doesn't agree, am I as open to his perception as I am to my idea that something special is happening? Can I be porous, completely open to the various frequencies?

What do we do with disagreement? In messianic and revelatory religious organizations you have constant struggle between the prophets. The head prophet gets bumped off by the new prophet and the group splinters, which looks a lot like the world we see around us, where the prophecy is about capitalism or military power. The sense of something greater than I am is a revelatory or mystical state that can be in disagreement with *your* revelatory state. What do we do with that?

We always construct the revelation with *me* as the prophet. We never construct the revelation with me as the nobody. The collective sense gets co-opted by individuation, and there's a constant interplay between the attempt to have our experience focused in a center and the *fact* that it's not really.

How do you know your perception is true? Perception is the sense of wholeness. Where the wholeness is going and what it's manifesting come into the sensibility of the individual, and there's the rub. What happens in that moment? Does it become me *having* the perception or does the perception take me with it wherever it goes? What I see is that perception actually destroys me. It's *never* what I think it's going to be, never what I thought it was going to be, never the projection at all. *It doesn't have anything to do with me.* This is the facing of personal destruction over and over and over again as it goes deeper and deeper and deeper.

Now I have the vision of God—*I* have it. Before I was a factory worker and I had a paycheck and it was about getting the money so I could go home and have my six-pack. *That* had to be destroyed, but now I've got the vision of God. I have to be destroyed in that too, it's the same thing. I never get to be the center. It's always being pulled away. It's an undulation happening simultaneously, but appearing to happen between the whole and the individuation. The nature of the individuation is to try to hold the vision to give itself location, but it's always being pulled out from under.

Physicists tell us that the particle is also a wave, and using this as an analogy for the individual and wholeness, we can say that the particle thinks the wave is something it holds. I, the particle, understand I'm located *here, I've* got the vision and you don't. The wave knows the particle's a wave, and that's what actually undermines. There's the resistance to that broadening, then there's the actual destruction of the particle, which really wasn't accurate to begin with. We're talking about a metaphorical particle/wave, but in fact it's neither a particle or a wave.

Is it possible to function in an integrated way, that is, to understand that although I function as an individual—I put on *my* shoes, I go to *my* car—at the same time the whole perceptual field is also happening. Is it possible to function in both, which is actually the fact? Or do we go back and forth?

Are we going to actually live as the wave and the particle or are we just going to talk about the possibility of living it? I think, "I'm ready for that life," and then that life actually starts to occur and I realize how *un*ready I am, because it doesn't fit my picture. *I* thought it was going to be about *me* saying profound things twenty-four hours a day, but what it's actually about is people saying profound things to *me* and then I have to take that in. My entire molecular structure has to restructure itself when everything in me says, "No, *I* want to be the one saying profound things." So it's completely wrong. I don't want to do that.

THE DESIGN OF LOVE

A relationship that is whole is going to wipe out the dream, the expectation, the projection—whatever the individual thinks they're getting out of it. Who can really stand in that particular fire? Who can enter into a relationship of love in which they don't get to be there, they don't get to enjoy the fruit? The only way the fruit is born is to not be there. Do you want that kind of relationship? *I* don't.

We think we know what falling in love means because we watch movies that tell us that somewhere on earth there's that special person who's created just for us. We organize our life around, "I want to love *you* because you're the kind of person that would really work for me. Me and you, that's love, but me and *her*, I don't think so." What I'm trying to draw from you in that case is really about me, it's really an ego draw, it isn't about you at all. There's no relationship to you, it's just my relationship to me.

Love is actually, "You're good for me and she's not, and I love you both."

The energy doesn't require something to happen but it does require the communication of it by living in it, speaking of it, designing everything from it. It does require humiliation. When you step into love by expressing it, you're taking the risk of being completely flattened. Something washes over the structure of what you are, which if you're resisting it, feels like getting knocked over. If you're not resisting, it just feels like energy. When you construct something in the face of it, it's like a hurricane knocking down the houses and the telephone poles. You think, "I don't want to have *my* house knocked down, so I'll control the situation by either deciding it's hopeless and I can't actually have that love, or by deciding I can have that love by formatting it in a particular way."

But if you don't resist, then what do you *do* with the energy? What if you overtly express and state that quality in your life? Do we actually express that in the design of our life? Or do we design our life to express it *only* where it's a safe thing, where it's a romantic love or it's a generalized love of life? What if we give expression to it? What if I just met you and I feel an amazing love energy and I don't know what it means but I still express it to you. What's your experience of that? You're going to react to it, laugh at it, think I'm really crazy, think I'm weird—this is the humiliation, the experience of being knocked over.

If I say I love you to a man, there are all kinds of responses conditioned into it. If I say I love you to a woman, there's also conditioning. Am I picking her up? What is happening? It doesn't leave me with any identity, because whatever the identity is it's going to be crushed. In a larger social structure, if we say our relationship as a group is about the moving energy, can we bear that? Can the world around us bear it? Will we become a cult? Will we become laughable? Will we live in some kind of bubble world? It's the same thing. Are we willing to stand in that?

The integration of the dual and non-dual worlds is to stand in the integration, and to not make it into an either/or perception. You think, "This is love because it's a church, because it's a marriage, because it's something society accepts," so you can be non-dual. But when you go to your job and there's the boss and the *you*—that's a dual world. Where is love?

What's the message of the dual world? What's the message of the pain of conflict and separation? Does the energy have movement or is it just still? Is it a snapshot or a movie? If the energy is moving, then something is starting to design itself, it's self-recognizing. This is why expression takes place. This is why we step into the risk, to find that which responds and begins to design.

If something's open and alive and has life to it, then that's the acknowledgement of love. It's the acknowledgement that we're in some energy and we don't know what it is. It's not like I need something from you or you need something from me. There's no particular acquisition taking place, there's just an open exploration. This is a different kind of romance or love affair, one that can simply exist as formless energy. It doesn't *need* to be anything.

It *can* take form, of course. Is it trying to design something? Is our romance a marriage? Shall we live together and produce progeny, take on a mortgage? What form does a romance that doesn't need form actually produce?

It can mutate, it can become whatever it is. It's a relationship that allows sharing and growing and moving together, in which the people don't *need* each other. There's no emptiness trying to be filled. If it's a marriage, what does that kind of marriage consist of? Do we go live in suburbia and get our two cars and our dog? Does that kind of marriage *want* that kind of form? What does the energy want to design? What kind of life comes from it?

But let's say I express to you immense love, and it doesn't require a form. You don't have to respond in any way to me at all, I'm just letting you know that. You say, "That's also true for me and there's no requirement." Then I think, this is a lot like a romance. I think I'm in love with *this* person, and this person needs to respond, so we fall into the form of things. But then I notice that you're not actually calling me back. Now I experience the pain of the non-response to the romantic relationship I've constructed out of just energy. And then I notice that it's just a construction, and I'm back in the energy. Then I think, but it would really be nice to be with her. What happens in that? Do I just go back and forth endlessly? Is this what we do?

Where's the integration?

We get stuck in the idea of going into the pain and coming out of the pain. We think that's the integration. Instead, what if we design something that is *not* the old relationship, that isn't a romantic movie from the Fifties we know isn't real? There isn't someone somewhere on earth who's going to be ready for me with the martini when I get home, and I'm not going to be the knight in shining armor who's going to protect her from life.

What does love energy design in human relationship? What kind of relationship could we have that is the integration of this energy and the fact of individuation? If I ask, "Would you like to discover that form with me?" and you say, "No, actually I'd like to have a Fifties type of relationship," I say fine—I still feel that love, but it has no form, because a Fifties relationship has no actuality for me. If instead you respond that you'd like to discover what our relationship is, then we have energy discovering form. That discovery is going to have to face the old form, and the constant movement towards something new, and the resistance. This is what a relationship is—a dynamic exploration of the movement of energy.

Love is What We Are

It usually seems to us that the love experience is generated by some particular person. We think our response to that person creates the feeling of all-encompassing love and the corresponding energy and creativity. However, we are constructing backwards from what's happening. If I meet you and I feel love, I say you and I are in love. You created this love in me, therefore I must have you. That's the way we construct it. But the way it happens is that a movement of expansion takes place and you *happen* to be in the environment. I think you caused it, but it's coincidental. Do we mutually recognize that energy, or do we mutually *identify* ourselves *as* that energy? What we usually do is to say I love you, do you love me, great, now we can love each other and *hold* that energy. In actuality, the movement is taking place, and if we both recognize that then we somehow explore the energy together, but we don't know what its form is.

When the coincidence of love happens, we think the particular form in it focuses the energy or makes it identifiable, but the opposite is actually taking place. The energy creates the form; the form doesn't create the energy. We turn it around because we want to be in control.

Are we living as energy creating the form? Or are we living as a form touching energy? Once we recognize that all of us are energy, and energy is creating these particular forms, then it becomes a question of design. As energy, what are we creating, what is the design? The question is not, "I am the design trying to get the energy, so how can I continue this design?" It's not, "How can I continue *me* by having *you*?" Instead, it's "I don't exist in separation, and you recognize that *you* don't exist either, and there's energy bubbling up in these forms, so what do these forms express?"

Form and formlessness are coincidental and intertwined. One doesn't exist without the other. Only in talking about it do we create the formless and the form. We make it about form because we think form is where it's at and anything else is adjunct to form.

Can I express to you the formlessness, understanding that it's almost universally likely that you're going to take it as only form? That you'll think I'm hitting on you. That you'll think I want you as my girlfriend or boyfriend. What I'm really asking you is, "Can you see that there's an intense energy taking place?" I have to find out whether you see that to explore it. If you *can't* see it, then it's going to move through form, which is likely to be either your repulsion about my advance or your attraction to that advance, and then I've got to move through *that* world.

If that construction doesn't happen, then we have

changeable form. We have an energetic relationship that happens to have forms in it. What do we do with that? Can you and I have a relationship that consistently and constantly recognizes energy, not form, as its basis?

The tension of all form in our personal relationships is that of whether they are embedded in the energetic reality or not. If not, then the relationship is going to become more and more about trying to maintain itself in form alone. This is conflict and pain and it can only fail, it can only go to destruction. It may take thirty years to do it, but if we don't anchor the relationship in the actuality, it will eventually crash and burn. Here's the risk though—if we anchor it in the energy, I may not get to have the romance with you. It may only destroy. I may recognize that energy with you and that creates jealousy with *him*. Now he wants to fight with you, and the world of form is trying to draw everything into itself and be all about form. I'm left with energy. I'm saying it's about the energy, it's about the energy, and everybody runs away, and I lose the whole show. I lost you and everything else. Then there's aloneness.

To face aloneness, what is required is to express connection and to take whatever the humiliation, whatever the destruction, and whatever the beauty that comes of that. Perhaps you and I recognize the energy *and* he recognizes it. Now we have a really interesting question, which is what's the form of three of us recognizing love energy? Or four of us, or ten of us? Does it become a tantric cult, does it become a church? What do we do with it?

We think the form is giving us what we really want. But if we recognize that I *am* the energy and *you're* the energy, we see that love is not what we need to get, love is what we are There's nothing to be afraid of, nothing to lose. You can't lose love by losing the form.

WHAT DO WE TRUST?

We're great deconstructionists, we've got that down. But can we step into the positive expression, the design, the construction? Or are we so mistrustful of construction that we think that anything we can construct *must* be some kind of aberration? The deconstruction, the negation, is the *easy* part. The riskier, more dangerous, more difficult part is the creation.

As an example, the school I helped to start had to construct itself somehow out of an ideal. We knew that the ideal couldn't stand the reality of life, the reality of children and staff and community, but somehow it had to move initially into form and be prepared to continue moving. And in fact it has. That requires letting go of what we thought it was, what we *knew* it was even, and stepping constantly into the unknown of what it can be. With that openness and the death of the ideal, new energy, people, and forces came into play, which is really what the school is about. It's about being a reflection of the moving question of what a learning community is. It requires a step into something that we know isn't complete.

In the beginning a lot of people said they wanted to create a school. But it was only when one person said, *"I'm* going to do this," as a focusing of that "we," that it actually began to take form. She didn't want to be the focal point. She wanted to help someone else who would be the initiator, but life chose her, in a way, because she was the only one available, so she reluctantly took it on. And it was only because she was later willing to step out of that role and to let it go that new "we" energy started coming in and new individuals moved into various roles. They *also* have to be prepared to let go so that new energy can come in.

It's not about what the individual wants; it's about what the movement of energy wants. Are we prepared to be the slave to the moving energy at the expense of our personal desires?

The nature of creativity is that you may get something that *looks* like what you want. But then what do you do with it? Do you let it become part of the movement or do you try to grab it and hold it for yourself?

What do we trust in the end? This is the fundamental question. Largely we trust in our ability to control the environment—to control you, control what you think of me, and to control how I present myself. Once you're gone and the door's closed, I can relax, but in the meantime it's all about control. When my ability to manage my relationship to you and what you think of me breaks down, as it does in all of our lives, then what do I actually trust? When that breaks down, things look really dark.

What happens when every aspect of my life I thought was working self-destructs? My marriage dissolves, my money is gone, my health disintegrates. Whatever I thought was giving me security, whatever I thought the future was, has evaporated. When things are okay, I can trust in my ability to manage. It *appears* that I'm managing my life because things are okay. But when things are completely out of control and all my management doesn't mean a thing, I'm faced with a more radical assessment of what it's all about, because everything I see, everything I know is broken. Is the universe broken in that moment, or are my ideas broken? If I'm holding on to trust in my ideas and projections, then it's a very dark place. If I'm introduced to a different kind of trust—a mystical trust, something I can't possibly *know* about, in fact, the breakdown of what is known—then this is a new world. It's not a dark world at all, it's really an unknown world, a world that's full of energy. Do I trust that energetic world? Do I trust the unknown?

What falls away is that you have a choice about trusting or not trusting. I'm asking it as a question, as a way of illustrating it or opening up the consideration. But I don't see that there's a choice. If there is, I'm still trying to control: "I think I'll trust life now because that looks like the better option." When you're completely obliterated—*including* any sense that you're controlling *anything,* even your choice whether or not to trust—you're just left in the energy. That's what remains.

We don't have the faintest idea of what constitutes a life that's "working," that's how unknown it is. In a way the concept *working* is no more relevant than the concepts *trust* or *choice.* In the energetic movement, the energy is all there is. It doesn't have a clear pathway. *Unknown* is useful only because it's a negative word. But is there something knowable about the energy? Is there something creative? Is there something patterned or directed in it? Does it have direction? Can it design?

About the Author

Steven Harrison is the author of:

Doing Nothing
Being One
Getting to Where You Are
The Question to Life's Answers
The Happy Child
What's Next After Now?
The Shimmering World

For more information: www.doingnothing.com or www.sentientpublications.com

Sentient Publications, LLC publishes books on cultural creativity, experimental education, transformative spirituality, holistic health, new science, ecology, and other topics, approached from an integral viewpoint. Our authors are intensely interested in exploring the nature of life from fresh perspectives, addressing life's great questions, and fostering the full expression of the human potential. Sentient Publications' books arise from the spirit of inquiry and the richness of the inherent dialogue between writer and reader.

Our Culture Tools series is designed to give social catalyzers and cultural entrepreneurs the essential information, technology, and inspiration to forge a sustainable, creative, and compassionate world.

We are very interested in hearing from our readers. To direct suggestions or comments to us, or to be added to our mailing list, please contact:

SENTIENT PUBLICATIONS, LLC
1113 Spruce Street
Boulder, CO 80302
303-443-2188
contact@sentientpublications.com
www.sentientpublications.com